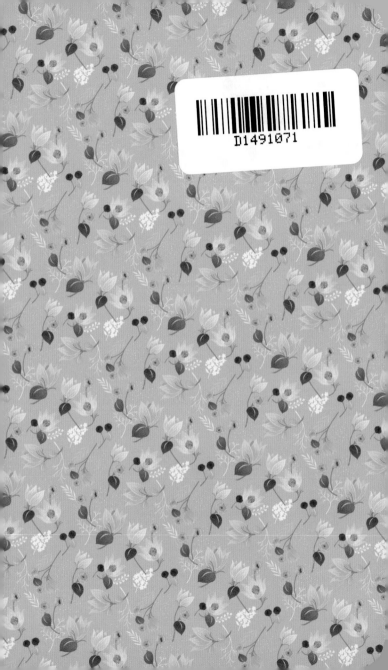

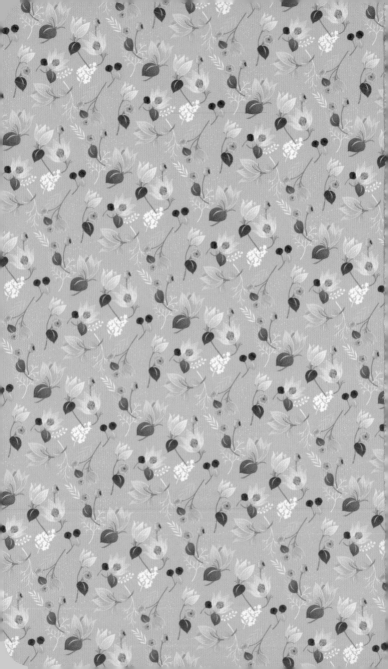

TO

_____

FROM

_____

DATE

_____

A Prayer a Day for Hope and Encouragement
Copyright © 2019 by DaySpring
First Edition, May 2019

Published by:

DaySpring
P.O. Box 1010
Siloam Springs, AR 72761
dayspring.com

Written by Lisa Stilwell
Designed by Gearbox
Typeset by Jessica Wei
Made in China
Prime: 91627
ISBN: 978-1-68408-679-5

REVIVAL OF THE HEART

The High and Exalted One who lives forever,
whose name is holy, says this:
"I live in a high and holy place, and with the
oppressed and lowly of spirit,
to revive the spirit of the lowly and revive
the heart of the oppressed."

ISAIAH 57:15

Father, Your presence is all around—from
the heights of the heavens to the bottoms
of the seas. You rejoice in my victories, and
You comfort me in my trials. Revive me in
the year ahead, Lord. Renew my strength
for the coming horizon. Heal my wounds
from last year's battles, and instill in me a
new passion for another year of serving You
in the fullness of Your joy. In Jesus' name.

AMEN.

TRUST IN HIM

Those who trust in the LORD will renew their
strength; they will soar on wings like eagles;
they will run and not become weary, they
will walk and not faint.

ISAIAH 40:31

Father, I confess I often trust in myself more
than I trust in You, and I am tired! Please
forgive me for putting You second. I look to
You this day and year ahead with full faith
and belief that You are with me and You
will help me with all that I am facing much
better than I can do on my own. Knowing
this gives me great peace, assurance, and
rest for my spirit, and I am grateful. In
Jesus' name.

AMEN.

NEW LIFE

Therefore, if anyone is in Christ, he is a new creation; the old has passed away, and see, the new has come!

II CORINTHIANS 5:17

Jesus, I am so thankful to know that, since accepting You as my Savior, I am no longer the lost and hopeless person I used to be. You have given me a new start, a clean slate, and a fresh beginning at life that I didn't know existed. I am Yours to do with as You will because I trust You and believe with all my heart that Your plans for me are good. To You be all glory.

AMEN.

A RENEWED SPIRIT

God, create a clean heart for me and renew
a steadfast spirit within me.

PSALM 51:10

Lord, I am so sorry for the ways I fall short
of saying and doing the right things. It's
hard not to let negative thoughts and
habits slide into each day. Please give me
a new and fresh determination to think
positively and act with pure motives that
are consistent with a testimony that honors
You. In Jesus' name.

AMEN.

PERFECT INSTRUCTION

The instruction of the Lord is perfect,
renewing one's life; the testimony of
the Lord is trustworthy, making the
inexperienced wise.

PSALM 19:7

O Lord, how I love Your Word and the
wisdom I gain each time I read it. There
are answers to my questions and countless
verses expressing Your faithful love for me.
But even more, when I read through the
pages, I hear from Your heart and get to
know You better each day. Thank You for
helping me navigate through the twists
and turns of my life. I would be lost without
Your instruction and help. In Your name.

AMEN.

INNER RENEWAL

Though our outer self is wasting away, our
inner self is being renewed day by day.
II CORINTHIANS 4:16 ESV

Lord, physical changes may reveal I'm
getting older, but in the light of Your love I
couldn't feel more alive and ready to face
each new day. Knowing and serving You
brings joy and strength with a steadfast
endurance deep within. It's an energy and
passion nothing else compares to. You are
an awesome God. In Your precious name.

AMEN.

FULFILLING HIS PURPOSE

Turn my eyes away from vanity [all those
worldly, meaningless things that distract—
let Your priorities be mine], and restore me
[with renewed energy] in Your ways.

PSALM 119:37 AMP

Yes, Lord, please do turn my eyes away
from all that doesn't matter in light of
eternity. Pursuing worldly gain saps my
energy, but fulfilling my purpose in You
gives renewed passion and strength. Guide
me in the way of Your truth and keep me in
the center of what matters most to You.

AMEN.

NEW BIRTH

He saved us because of His mercy, and not
because of any good things that we have
done. God washed us by the power of the
Holy Spirit. He gave us new birth and a
fresh beginning.

TITUS 3:5 CEV

Father, I know that only because of
Your mercy and grace I can live free and
empowered through Your Spirit within me.
The past no longer has power to influence
or control my thoughts and actions; new
life in You is now my focus and wellspring
of life. For this, I lift all praise to You.

AMEN.

NEW MIRACLES

So the crowd marveled as they saw the
mute speaking, the crippled restored, and
the lame walking, and the blind seeing; and
they glorified the God of Israel.

MATTHEW 15:31 NASB

Lord, You are a God of miracles. Whether
physical, emotional, relational, or spiritual,
You repair broken pieces and make them
whole. I ask today for Your compassion
to reach down and work in my life—to
heal the bruises I carry in my heart and
to fill me with Your peace that passes all
understanding. Revive Your Spirit within
me so it burns with a flame that cannot be
quenched, no matter what I face.

In Jesus' name.

AMEN.

LIVE IN TODAY

Because of the LORD's faithful love we do
not perish, for His mercies never end.
They are new every morning;
great is Your faithfulness!
LAMENTATIONS 3:22-23

Lord, thank You that every morning is a
fresh new start—for walking in obedience to
You, for blessing others who cross my path,
for praying for those who need a prayer,
and for embracing Your holy presence in
my life. Yesterday is over and behind. Help
me to move forward and live this day in the
fullness of Your grace.

AMEN.

TRANSFORMED FROM WITHIN

Put to death what belongs to your earthly nature...You are being renewed in knowledge according to the image of your Creator.

COLOSSIANS 3:5,10

Father, I want to stop responding to old, unhealthy habits and start living in a way that shows You are the whole of my life and the reason I live. Make Your ways the desire of my heart, and give me strength to overcome the strongholds that have kept me from experiencing true freedom in You. In Christ's name I pray.

AMEN.

CLEANSED FROM SIN

Be gracious to me, God, according to Your faithful love; according to Your abundant compassion, blot out my rebellion. Completely wash away my guilt and cleanse me from my sin.

PSALM 51:1-2

Father, I confess to You and ask Your forgiveness for the ways I try to live for myself instead of for You. Why do I continually get off track and do things my way instead of looking to You first? Please forgive me and cleanse my heart. I want to be ever so sensitive to the leading of Your Spirit and carry a willingness to do, say, and go Your way—whatever You ask. In Jesus' name I pray.

AMEN.

HE REVIVES THE SPIRIT

Your righteousness reaches heaven, God,
You who have done great things;
God, who is like You? You caused me to
experience many troubles and misfortunes,
but You will revive me again.
You will bring me up again,
even from the depths of the earth.

PSALM 71:19-20 HCSB

Lord, I don't always understand why You
allow hardship in my life, but I choose to
trust You. I believe You to be a good Father,
and I know that You are with me. I walk in
faith that You will redeem what I think is
lost, and that You will revive my spirit with
renewed strength, purpose, and meaning—
all for Your glory. In Jesus' name.

AMEN.

A NEW MIND

Do not be conformed to this age, but be transformed by the renewing of your mind, so that you may discern what is the good, pleasing, and perfect will of God.

ROMANS 12:2

Father, I confess I get distracted by the voices of this world that pull me away from You and Your will for my life. It's a battle not to be fought on my own logic and ideas. Please, drown out anything that is not of You. I want to hear Your voice and know just what You want and have for me this day. Fill me with Your wisdom and guide my steps so I am walking close to You. In Jesus' name.

AMEN.

TODAY IS A NEW DAY

Have nothing to do with your old sinful life.
It was sinful because of being fooled into
following bad desires. Let your minds and
hearts be made new.

EPHESIANS 4:22-23 NLV

Lord, help me to turn away from the
memories of my past and dispel the
thoughts that bring any heaviness of
shame. Today is a new day, and knowing
You means knowing freedom from the
bondage of when I was lost. I claim my
freedom now and pray that You guard my
heart and mind from the enemy's attempts
to rob me of the peace that You give. I walk
afresh today with You in my sights. Thank
You, Jesus, for giving me true freedom.
In Your name I pray.

AMEN.

A CLEAN HEART

As a face is reflected in water,
so the heart reflects the real person.
PROVERBS 27:19 NLT

Father, I want my life to reflect a pure
and clean heart that loves You. Show me
any ways I am not being true to You or to
myself. Help me to examine my motives for
the things I do and the conversations I have.
Give me a humble heart that is fueled by a
desire to serve and pray for others. Guard
my heart from selfishness. Mend my heart
so it's whole and strong and filled with Your
joy. Help me to reflect Your love all around
so that others are drawn to You.
In Your name I pray.
AMEN.

NEW HEIGHTS OF TRUST

Early in the morning before the sun is up,
I am praying and pointing out how much I
trust in You.

PSALM 119:147 TLB

O Lord, how I love You. I come to You this
day releasing my anxious thoughts and
entrusting my needs to Your care. You have
provided so abundantly in the past; please
increase my faith to trust You more than
ever with my cares for the future. Fill me
with Your peace that passes understanding,
and help me walk through this day in full
confidence that I can trust You completely
with every detail. To You, Jesus, I pray.

AMEN.

A NEW WORK

For it is God who works in you to will and
to act in order to fulfill His good purpose.

PHILIPPIANS 2:13 NIV

Lord, help me to apply Your Word to my
everyday life. Help me make this a discipline
of the mind and heart, empowered by Your
Spirit, transforming me each day more and
more into Your likeness. Keep me on Your
path of righteousness and help me to fulfill
the purposes You have just for me.
In Jesus' name I pray.

AMEN.

A NEW START

You were washed, you were sanctified, you were justified in the name of the Lord Jesus Christ and by the Spirit of our God.

I CORINTHIANS 6:11 NIV

Father, I am so grateful to You for sending Your Son and displaying the most beautiful act of love known to the world. Because of Jesus' sacrifice, I am made clean and whole—my transgressions no longer have a hold on me. I am free of sin's stain, I am sealed by Your Spirit within, and I worship and praise Your name for such a gift. Thank You for the assurance of Your faithful love and healing grace.

AMEN.

WASHED CLEAN

Let us come near to God with a sincere heart and a sure faith, with hearts that have been purified from a guilty conscience and with bodies washed with clean water.

HEBREWS 10:22 GNT

Lord, I come to You today with a humble and sincere heart, praising Your work and supremacy in my life. The power of Your Spirit to clear my conscience makes me a walking miracle. I look to You now and walk in faith that You are with me, pouring into me Your love and grace and newness of heart. In Jesus' name.

AMEN.

A CLEAN HEART

And God, who knows the heart, bore
witness to them by giving them the Holy
Spirit...cleansing their hearts by faith.

ACTS 15:8-9

Lord, thank You for the gift of Your Holy
Spirit. I want this year to be a time of going
where Your Spirit leads and living in the
abundance of Your grace. Cleanse my heart
of all that would hinder Your voice or cause
me to stumble. I want only to see and hear
You above all else. All praise be to You.

AMEN.

HE KNOWS THE FUTURE

The Lord will always lead you,
satisfy you in a parched land,
and strengthen your bones. You will
be like a watered garden and like a spring
whose water never runs dry.

ISAIAH 58:11

Father, sometimes life on this earth is hard.
Thinking on this new year ahead, I can't
see how plans will turn out. But I put Your
face in the view of whatever is ahead,
and I trust that You will provide as You've
promised in Your Word. Please go before
me. Lead me so that no matter how difficult
circumstances may get, I have steadfast
hope and assurance that I will remain in
Your care. I love You and thank You
for Your goodness.

AMEN.

HIS WELLSPRING OF LIFE

[The people] are filled from the abundance
of your house. You let them drink
from Your refreshing stream.
For the wellspring of life is with You.

PSALM 36:8-9

Lord, You are a wellspring of life to draw
from each and every day. And as I draw
from You, I am renewed—with new hope,
new strength, and new eyes to see just
how almighty You are. Thank You for filling
me with the blessing of Your joy and the
warmth of Your love. In Jesus' name.

AMEN.

A NEW SONG

I waited patiently for the Lord, and he
turned to me and heard my cry for help.
He brought me up from a desolate pit...
making my steps secure. He put a new song
in my mouth, a hymn of praise to our God.

PSALM 40:1-3

Father, I am so filled with praise for
You today. When I look back at where
You've brought me, I am amazed at the
transformation of my life. You raised me up
from despair and placed me in the embrace
of Your loving arms. In You I have hope and
peace that wells up so much, I cannot stop
praising You. Thank You for putting a new
song in my heart.

AMEN.

A NEW WORK

Lord, You are our Father; we are the clay,
and You are our potter; we all are the work
of Your hands.

ISAIAH 64:8

Lord, my life is Yours. Mold me, shape me,
develop me into a work with which You are
well pleased. I want my life to reveal the
work of Your hands and the power of what
You, as almighty God, can and will do. Use
me for furthering Your kingdom to the lost,
and for inspiring others who know You.
Make me a vessel that can stand the heat
and pressures that are sure to come, as well
as a place where Your love can flow out
freely from within. To You be all glory.

AMEN.

NO MORE STAIN

All the prophets testify about Him, that through His name everyone who believes in Him [whoever trusts in and relies on Him, accepting Him as Savior and Messiah] receives forgiveness of sins.

ACTS 10:43 AMP

Heavenly Father, I trust in You. I believe that Jesus died for my sins and covers me now with His grace. It's a gift to know that when I confess my sin, Your mercy reaches down and removes the stain and weight it could otherwise leave. You give me hope for a future in eternity with You, and for this my heart rejoices at the sound of Your name.

AMEN.

RENEWED HOPE

When doubts filled my mind, Your comfort
gave me renewed hope and cheer.

PSALM 94:19 NLT

Lord, Your faithful love is a lifeline for me.
Sometimes doubt pours into my mind
because I can't see how circumstances
will turn out, and I don't know what to do
except call on You. So I'm calling out to
You now. Please hear my cry and surround
me with Your peace. Forgive me for ever
doubting Your ability to work out all things
for my good and Your glory. I want to soak
in the comfort You so willingly provide and
rest in renewed hope as I trust in You.
All praise to You.

AMEN.

GENUINE FULFILLMENT

If you continue in My word, you really are
My disciples. You will know the truth, and
the truth will set you free.

JOHN 8:31-32

O Father, I want and need Your truth. I want
to follow Your ways and live according to
Your holy standards. It's so easy and often
tempting to be fooled by the world's road
to happiness, yet Your Word shines brightly
the truths on which to live and the promises
You've given for genuine fulfillment. Where
Your Spirit is, there is new freedom every
day. With praise and thanksgiving.

AMEN.

NEW PATHS

A person's heart plans his way,
but the Lord determines his steps.

PROVERBS 16:9

Yes, Lord, I have plans for the year ahead,
but I want You to be the Master of them
all. Show me which ones to pursue and
which to disregard, which to nurture and
which to put away for another time. I want
Your way to shine brighter than the steps
I've set out for myself, so I put both palms
up and release to You my will in exchange
for Yours. Have Your way with me, Lord. In
Jesus' name.

AMEN.

REDEEMING GRACE

Our Father in heaven, your name be
honored as holy. Your kingdom come.
Your will be done on earth as it is in heaven.
MATTHEW 6:9-10

Father, I honor Your name and look to
Your will for my life. Help me to live out
one day at a time in light of Your overall
plans, not just for me but for this world
and the chaotic state of humanity. I pray
in reverence and awe as I look at Your
Son, Jesus, and the redeeming grace He
provides. I confess I am nothing without
You, yet with You, I can live in complete
victory. Hallelujah! I lift my praise and
worship to Your holy name.
AMEN.

HE REBUILDS

After you have suffered for a little while, the
God of all grace, the One who called you
into His eternal glory in Christ Jesus, will
Himself restore, empower, strengthen,
and establish you.

I PETER 5:10 CEB

Lord, I am so grateful to know that no
matter what's been lost due to my failed
health, my mistakes, or someone else's
actions, You are a redeeming God. You
promise to rebuild and empower, refresh
and make new for Your continued purpose.
I entrust my circumstances to You and live
forward in new grace and new mercy as You
establish my feet on unshakable ground.
In Jesus I pray.

AMEN.

FEBRUARY

LOVE

THE FULLNESS OF HIS LOVE

I want you to know all about Christ's love, although it is too wonderful to be measured. Then your lives will be filled with all that God is.

EPHESIANS 3:19 CEV

Father, You are greater than life. No other source of love has filled my heart, soul, and mind the way Yours has. It is so great, I cannot comprehend it all. And I know Your love is sincere and eternal as it points to Jesus' death on the cross for me. I am forever grateful for Your sacrificial love.

AMEN.

COMPLETE LOVE

Love the LORD your God
with all your heart, with all your soul,
and with all your strength.
DEUTERONOMY 6:5 GNT

Lord, I put You on the throne of my heart
and look up to You with all the love I
can imagine. I know this means putting
my wants and plans down and living
completely for You. And I know I fall short
of this, sometimes daily, yet because of
Your great love, I know I am forgiven, which
makes me love You even more. You are a
Father to the fatherless, a Husband to the
widow, a Friend to those who know You,
and a Savior to a lost and hopeless world.
All praise be to You.
AMEN.

GLIMPSES OF HIS LOVE

Your steadfast love is before my eyes,
and I walk in faithfulness to You.
PSALM 26:3 NRSV

Father, I look around and see touches of
Your love everywhere. Your provision, Your
protection, Your healing, and Your saving
grace—Your presence is abundant. I walk
in faithfulness to You today, knowing and
trusting that I am Your child, and that You
reign in my life. I open my mouth with
praise and thanksgiving, and I open my
heart to let in Your love, today and every
day. I remain committed to Your ways and
walk in faithfulness to You. In Christ's name.
AMEN.

JEALOUS LOVE

The LORD your God, who is among you,
is a jealous God.

DEUTERONOMY 6:15

Father, it is sometimes hard to fathom that
You are right here with me. You, God, are
with me when I rise, when I work, when I
sleep, when I pray. You hear my thoughts
and eagerly receive my prayers. Thank
You for such a height of love that You are
jealous when too much of my attention
goes to people and things that don't fulfill
or complete me as You do. Your warm
embrace is where I want to be.

AMEN.

SPEAKING LOVE

Praising and cursing come out of the same
mouth. My brothers, these things should
not be this way.... Can a fig tree produce
olives...or a grapevine produce figs?
Neither can a saltwater spring
yield fresh water.

JAMES 3:10-12 HCSB

Lord, I know that gossip, bad words, and
criticism are all contrary to the love You tell
me to have for my neighbors. Please put a
guard and filter over my mouth, and help
me to speak only what is edifying, uplifting,
and encouraging to those around me. Help
me to see the good in others the way You
do. Help me to highlight that which will
bless another heart and make someone
else's day.

AMEN.

MOTIVATED BY LOVE

Let everything you do be done in love
[motivated and inspired
by God's love for us].
I CORINTHIANS 16:14 AMP

Father, as I go through this day, help me
to have pure motives in my actions and
words. Help me to put "self" aside and
really see the needs around me. Give me
a heart of compassion for reaching out
and truly loving others through service or
encouragement, even if all I do is make eye
contact and give a smile. Help me to make
a difference in how others see You—the
exalted and omnipotent God of love. Praise
to Your holy name.

AMEN.

HIS LOVE IS THERE

Blessed be the LORD, for he has wondrously
shown his faithful love to me
in a city under siege.

PSALM 31:21

Lord, this world can be frightening—
headlines read of attacks and killings, and
chaos is rampant. It seems that wherever I
look, there is a city or family under siege.
And yet Your love abounds. It shines
brighter than my best of days and is a
beacon of hope on the scary ones. Your
love is there for whenever and however I
need, and for this I am grateful.

AMEN.

LOVE YOUR ENEMIES

But I say to you, Love your enemies and
pray for those who persecute you.
MATTHEW 5:44 ESV

O Lord, this is Your command, but I confess
it's hard. Help me, please, to actually do
it. The next time I'm tempted to retaliate
toward someone who's offended me,
remind me to love. Help me to remember
that there's always a bigger plan with a
deeper meaning than what I see in any
given moment. And help me to remember
the ultimate example of love You showed
when You died on the cross for all of
humanity. In Your name I pray.
AMEN.

START WITH LOVE

But the Spirit produces love, joy, peace,
patience, kindness, goodness, faithfulness,
humility, and self-control.

GALATIANS 5:22-23 GNT

Lord, it is obvious I cannot love on my
own—it comes from You and the power
of Your Spirit within me. So if I want more
love, I simply need more of You. Please
hear me now and fill my thoughts with Your
truth. Help me to share Your love from the
overflow of Your presence. I want to exude
all the fruit of the Spirit, but love is where it
begins, so I begin this day with You.
I love You, Jesus.

AMEN.

THE FATHER'S LOVE

See what great love the Father has given us
that we should be called God's children—
and we are!

I JOHN 3:1

Father, it's no less than amazing to think
that I am Your child. Baggage, problems,
hang-ups, bad habits and all, You took me
in and now call me Your own. I have been
adopted into Your family and sealed with
the promise of hope and a future. Thank
You for loving me enough to include me in
Your royal lineage. My heart is glad, and I
rejoice in Your presence in my life as I live
and grow in Your family. In Jesus' name.

AMEN.

WITHOUT LOVE

If I speak human or angelic tongues
but do not have love, I am a noisy gong
or a clanging cymbal.

I CORINTHIANS 13:1

Lord, I know that I can help the homeless,
serve a neighbor, and say prayers on behalf
of the hurting, but if I don't do any of these
with a sincere heart of love, the effects
can fall short of what could be. The point
of reaching out to the lost, even other
Christians, is to spread Your love and point
people to You, not to boost my image or
make me look good. Convict my heart
when love is not at the core and in the
lead. I want to keep You at the forefront of
whatever I say or do.

AMEN.

OBEDIENT LOVE

Love means doing what God has
commanded us, and He has commanded us
to love one another.

II JOHN 6 NLT

Father, if I say I love You, that means I
should willingly do what You say to do.
It means putting Your will and Your way
above mine and really seeing the needs of
others around me. But I get so busy and
preoccupied, I don't see. And sometimes
I see but don't have the time to stop and
really love on someone who is hurting. I
know that loving others helps them and
brings You glory, but there's more: I am also
blessed in ways that my checked-off to-do
list will never compare to. Help me to fully
love today, Lord. In Your name I pray.

AMEN.

SUSTAINING LOVE

As God's ministers, we commend ourselves
in everything: by great endurance,
by afflictions, by hardships...by purity,
by knowledge, by patience, by kindness...
by sincere love.

II CORINTHIANS 6:4-6

Father, this verse reminds me of the song
"They Will Know We Are Christians by
Our Love." Allowing Your Spirit to do the
unexplainable, sustaining me through
great hardship, by sincerely loving others,
especially the unlovable, all bring attention
to You and the Christian faith. Help me
to remember this. Fill me with Your love
overflowing so that I can share it with
others to the point of standing out
for Your glory.

AMEN.

SACRIFICIAL LOVE

For God loved the world in this way:
He gave His one and only Son, so that
everyone who believes in Him will not
perish but have eternal life.

JOHN 3:16

Your love, O Lord, surpasses all other loves
in life. To sacrifice Your Son as an offering
for my sins is the greatest love gift of
all. Words cannot describe my heartfelt
thanks—for giving me new life here on earth
and eternal life in heaven with You. I am so
honored and humbled, blessed and filled
with nothing but praise for You.
I exalt Your name.

AMEN.

UNSHAKABLE LOVE

"Though the mountains move and the hills shake, My love will not be removed from you and My covenant of peace will not be shaken," says your compassionate LORD.

ISAIAH 54:10

Father, there are times when life moves and shakes the ground from underneath my feet and all I can do is hang on. It is so very comforting to know that no matter how big the quakes or how strong the tremors, Your love remains the same, and it is secure within my heart. I'm truly thankful to know that Your love is always there.
It sustains my will to keep going.
All thanks and praise be to You.

AMEN.

THE COVER OF LOVE

Hatred stirs up conflicts,
but love covers all offenses.

PROVERBS 10:12

Father, with all the conflict in news
headlines today, this truth rings louder and
clearer than ever. Help me take Your high
road to love, even when I'm offended or
disagree. Help me to love instead of lash,
to be silent instead of spew. I want to be
peace on Your behalf and have a heart of
love—Your love—so that the evidence of
Your grace will be seen by all. I ask this in
the name and power of Jesus.

AMEN.

CHOSEN LOVE

God loves you and has chosen you as His
own special people. So be gentle, kind,
humble, meek, and patient.
COLOSSIANS 3:12 CEV

Lord, to know that I am special to You
fills my heart to overflowing. When I stop
to bask in the warmth of Your presence,
I am overcome with peace that passes
understanding. Keep my heart humble.
Instill in me the kindness You would show
the hurting. Help me stay in Your sweet
spot of love so the fruit of gentleness and
patience will be an outpouring of blessing
to others. All glory to You, Jesus.
AMEN.

FAITHFUL LOVE

May Your faithful love rest on us, LORD,
for we put our hope in You.
PSALM 33:22

Father, the thought of Your love resting
on me brings such calm to my soul. And
it's much needed with so much unrest that
comes from the world and life in general.
There is no other option in my heart and
mind than to keep looking to You and
drawing from the love that You give in such
abundance. You are ever present in my life,
and I love You for Your faithfulness to me.
You are worthy of all praise.

AMEN.

HIS LOVINGKINDNESS

As for me, I shall sing of Your strength;
yes, I shall joyfully sing of Your
lovingkindness in the morning, for You
have been my stronghold and a refuge
in the day of my distress.

PSALM 59:16 NASB

Lord, I look to You and my heart is filled
with gladness. You have been good and
faithful to provide, protect, comfort, and
bring favor to all corners of my life. You put
a new song in my mouth, and I am filled
with praise and thanksgiving. I want the
world to know that Your love is life itself—
nothing else compares.
In Your holy name I pray.

AMEN.

GENTLE LOVE

For the kingdom of God is not a matter
of talk but of power. What do you want?
Should I come to you with a rod, or in love
and a spirit of gentleness?

I CORINTHIANS 4:20-21

Lord, this is easy to answer—I want Your
love and a spirit of gentleness! You are love,
and love is power—the greatest force in all
of humanity. When I wrong someone, I want
to be corrected with gentleness, so help
me to extend the same response to others
who offend me. Help me to stop talking and
start doing, to stop knowing in my head
and start acting from my heart.
Let love rule. In Jesus' name.

AMEN.

EXPRESSIONS OF LOVE

My lips will glorify You because
Your faithful love is better than life.

PSALM 63:3

Father, Your love is faithful—it is always
there to hold me together, no matter the
time of day or night. Many times I don't
even deserve it, yet it is there. You love me
even when I don't always love You back,
which is humbling. So I will praise You
openly and audibly; I sing songs of worship
to express the best that I can the immense
joy You bring to my heart. You deserve all
glory. You alone are worthy.

AMEN.

HIS LOVE IS PATIENT

Love is patient.

I CORINTHIANS 13:4

Lord, I'm so grateful for Your patience
when I lag behind or am slow to respond
to certain convictions. So often I hear You
telling me to do things, yet I get around
to them when I feel like it rather than
when You say. At the same time, I'm guilty
of being impatient with my family and
coworkers—they don't move fast enough
to fit my schedule. Please help me to be
patient and kind toward others today to
the same degree that I need patience and
kindness myself. Keep my heart humble
and help me to remember that love has the
power to heal the most stressful and broken
situations. In Your name.

AMEN.

WHAT LOVE IS NOT

Love...is not boastful,
is not arrogant, is not rude.

I CORINTHIANS 13:4-5

O Lord, when I am honest with myself, I
know there are times I boast about my
accomplishments and think a bit too highly
of myself. And I think the sum of both is
the epitome of rudeness. Please forgive
me for being the opposite of what I know
You want me to be. Please remove any
pride and replace it with pure and simple
humility and a quickness to give You the
glory where glory is due. All I have and all
I'm able to do is because of Your love and
grace over my life. With gratefulness I pray.

AMEN.

LOVE PUTS HIM FIRST

[Love] is not self-seeking.

I CORINTHIANS 13:5

Father, there is a constant battle within
to do my will rather than Yours. I want to
go my way, fulfill my dreams, and do it all
on my timeline. But it's a battle because I
sincerely want to seek Your will and fulfill
Your calling and purpose. Please help me
put self aside and remain focused with a
full heart of obedience to serve You and
put others' needs before mine. And help me
to truly trust that Your ways hold blessing
beyond what I could ever accomplish for
myself. In Jesus' name.

AMEN.

LOVE IS A CLEAN SLATE

[Love] does not keep a record of wrongs.
I CORINTHIANS 13:5

Father, I am so thankful and relieved that
ungodly things I did years ago, or even
as recent as yesterday, are forgiven—You
don't hold them over my head. They
are wiped away and forgotten. This is a
concept that's hard to fully grasp, because
I do the opposite—I often keep records of
how others have wronged me. Help me to
forgive and look forward, not backward.
Help me to extend the same grace to others
that You extend to me.
In the power of Jesus I pray.
AMEN.

LOVE IS TRUTH

Love...rejoices in the truth.
I CORINTHIANS 13:6

Lord, there are so many conflicting
messages this world sends, sometimes my
mind literally freezes—I don't know what
to think. I get unsure and insecure and
sometimes even depressed. This is why I
need and love Your Word—it is full of truth.
You are truth. And the more I know You,
the more I thrive and rejoice in the power
and freedom You give. Even when You
convict me of a sin or pull me to a place of
growth I don't want to go, my heart is full
of integrity and strength knowing I live and
stand in truth. All praise be to You.

AMEN.

LOVE BEARS ALL THINGS

[Love] bears all things.
I CORINTHIANS 13:7

Father, sometimes life gets very hard and I want to give up. I struggle to tolerate the shortcomings of others, and sometimes it seems easier to flee. But loves stays. Love bears all things—the way You stay and cover me in all the ways I fall short of Your purposes for me. Thank You for holding on to me and promising never to let go. Humble my heart and help me to display the same act of love toward others that You show toward me. In Jesus' name.

AMEN.

LOVE NEVER ENDS

Love never ends.

I CORINTHIANS 13:8

Father, what a blessing to know that Your
love never ends—it lasts through to eternity.
It's almost a foreign concept in a world
where people love each other one day, then
hate and leave each other the next. Nothing
is permanent here, not even love. Yet You
are love, and You are eternal. Today I will
rest in this promise and let my heart be
filled to the brim. In Jesus' love I pray.

AMEN.

SINCERE LOVE

Above all, maintain constant love
for one another, since love covers
a multitude of sins.

I PETER 4:8

Lord, help me to live out this day in Your
love. As I work, shop, drive, and eat, help
me to remain in a spirit of love toward each
person I greet. Help me to be all there with
each encounter and to extend grace the
same way You so lavishly drape it over me.
Help me to keep love as the goal higher
than any box I need to check on my to-do
list. In Your faithful love I pray.

AMEN.

MARCH

HOPE

HOPE IN THE LORD

Love the LORD, all His faithful ones.
The LORD protects the loyal,
but fully repays the arrogant. Be strong,
and let your heart be courageous,
all you who put your hope in the LORD.
PSALM 31:23–24

Lord, I love that when my hope is in You, I
am supernaturally filled with a strength and
courage like no other. That's because You
are unfailing and immovable—no weapon
fashioned against me can stand. As I go
through this day and look to You, I hold my
head and my heart high in the power of
Your name and the safety of Your care.
In Jesus' name.
AMEN.

HOPE DOESN'T
DISAPPOINT

We also rejoice in our afflictions, because
we know that affliction produces
endurance, endurance produces proven
character, and proven character produces
hope. This hope will not disappoint us.

ROMANS 5:3-5

Father, in my challenges and fears,
hardships and unknowns, hope is my
constant companion. This is because You
are with me—I know this full well. And
knowing You are with me—working Your
good, showing Your provision, and growing
me into the person You want—brings great
comfort to my heart. Each moment I dwell
on Your love and faithfulness, hope grows
deeper into my heart and stronger into my
spirit. My hope is in You. All praise to You.

AMEN.

HOPE FOR THE FUTURE

"I know what I have planned for you," says the LORD. "I have plans to prosper you, not to harm you. I have plans to give you a future filled with hope."

JEREMIAH 29:11 NET

Father, I am so comforted and assured to know that You know the plans for my life, because when I think of the future, it's easy to be anxious from all the unknowns. I don't know how problems of today will turn out for tomorrow, but You do, and I trust You. Your wellspring of mercy and spirit of grace are in my heart and evident in my life; I will not be afraid. My hope remains steadfast in You and no other. In Jesus' name my lips shall praise.

AMEN.

HOPE BELIEVES

[Abraham] believed, hoping against hope,
so that he became the father of many
nations according to what had been
spoken: So will your descendants be. He did
not weaken in faith.

ROMANS 4:18-19

Father, Abraham is so inspiring because He
believed You against all odds. When You
promised Him a son in his old age, he could
have focused on the impossibility, but he
didn't. He believed. Help me to have the
same faith and hope in Your Word that he
possessed deep within his heart. I claim the
same unwavering hope—yes, I believe—for
my life today. In Christ I pray.

AMEN.

HOPE FOR
A BROKEN WORLD

Maintain love and justice,
and always put your hope in God.
HOSEA 12:6

Lord, there is so much injustice on this
earth, it's hard at times not to lose hope.
Poverty, abuse, trafficking, crime, officials,
even some pastors I've looked up to have
so often disappointed. So I turn to You, the
One true source of hope for a very broken
world. Your faithfulness keeps my hope
burning for a better day and for strength to
do my part to help make a difference. You
are my God, and You are a God of hope.
All praise be to Jesus.
AMEN.

THE HOPE OF SALVATION

We should stay sober and in control,
covered with a breastplate of faith and love
and a helmet of the hope of salvation.
I THESSALONIANS 5:8 VOICE

Father, if there's one way the enemy tries
to rob me of hope, it's through my mind.
He works his way in and whispers words
of discouragement and defeat and fills me
with discouragement. But, thanks be to
Your Spirit within me, I don't have to listen.
Help me to take captive my thoughts to
the truths in Your Word—truths of love and
forgiveness, power and eternal life with You.
Guard my head and my heart, keeping life
and hope alive and untouchable.
In Jesus' name I pray.
AMEN.

THE HOPE
OF HIS CALLING

I pray that the eyes of your heart may be
enlightened so that you may know
what is the hope of His calling.

EPHESIANS 1:18

Lord, because of You and the great love
You have shown me, my heart is alive to
the hope of Your calling. I know that each
day is a chance to get closer to fulfilling the
purpose You have for me until I am at home
with You. Until that time, I rejoice in what
lies ahead each day until I reach the finish
line of my life and rise up to an eternal and
glorious future in Your presence.
I love You, Abba Father.

AMEN.

FALSE HOPE

Instruct those who are rich in the present
age not to be arrogant or to set their hope
on the uncertainty of wealth, but on God.

I TIMOTHY 6:17

Father, living in a society that says to place
my hope in financial gain is hard. Most
people seem to strive toward having more
things and building up their bank accounts.
Yet I know that You are the only source of
security in all forms. All that I have comes
from You, and Your provision is perfect.
Help me to remember that my needs
are met—I shall not want. And that Your
provision is for my enjoyment, not to fret
over. You've been so faithful;
my hope is in You only.

AMEN.

WHERE HOPE COMES FROM

Oh, I must find rest in God only, because my
hope comes from Him! Only God is my rock
and my salvation—my stronghold!—
I will not be shaken.

PSALM 62:5-6 CEB

Lord, life can be so full of challenges and
demands. I need Your help knowing what
to do and how to best handle them. I refuse
to retreat or be overwhelmed by the weight
of it all. Hold me in Your mighty right hand
and give me rest—sweet, peaceful rest. Give
me clarity of mind, courage for taking my
next steps, and Your supernatural strength
to sustain me in whatever circumstances I
face. Because of You, I will not be shaken.
To You be all the glory.

AMEN.

PURIFYING HOPE

Beloved...everyone who has this hope
fixed on Him purifies himself,
just as He is pure.

I JOHN 3:2-3 NASB

Jesus, what a blessing to dwell on the
goodness that comes from the hope found
in You. As I look at You, abide in You, focus
on You, walk with You...the benefits are too
great to comprehend. To be as pure as You
is beyond imagination, yet Your Word says
it's true. So through the power and love of
Your Spirit, purify my soul now, Lord. Make
me clean, wash me anew, and seal my life
with the Spirit of Your holiness and the joy
of Your salvation to come.
In Your holy name I pray.

AMEN.

THE GOSPEL OF HOPE

And now I [Paul] stand on trial
because of the hope in what God promised
to our ancestors.

ACTS 26:6

Father, the persecution of Christians around
the world is nothing new. The name of Jesus
alone can be a target for harassment and stir
all-out war in some countries. Yet thousands
have willingly stood the test of faith and been
imprisoned, beaten, and killed on behalf of
spreading Your gospel of hope to the lost.
Help me to remember that sharing this hope
is the most important thing I can ever do. And
that no matter how or where You lead me to
do this, You promise to be with me. I am a
soldier for Christ with all hope of bringing one
more person to the cross of life.
All honor and glory to You.

AMEN.

HOPE IN WHAT'S TO COME

The plowman ought to plow in hope,
and the thresher to thresh in hope
of sharing the harvest.

I CORINTHIANS 9:10 AMP

Lord, to plant a garden without the hope
of a harvest seems so pointless, yet that
is what the lost do every day. Without
salvation at the end of life's journey, what is
the point of living? I am so grateful for Your
pursuit of me, for blessing me with the gift
of new hope, and for a future of eternity
in Your presence. Help me to spread the
Word, to share the gospel with those I
meet who are secretly searching for more
meaning and purpose, and to help them
find the hope they need—You. Help me be a
missionary for You, Jesus.
In Your sweet name I pray.

AMEN.

HOPE FOR
WHAT'S NOT SEEN

Now in this hope we were saved, but hope that
is seen is not hope, because who hopes for
what he sees? Now if we hope for what we do
not see, we eagerly wait for it with patience.

ROMANS 8:24–25

Lord, not knowing the future can be unsettling,
especially when I look at circumstances. But
keeping You in front of me—step by step, day
by day—keeps hope alive. I believe with all my
heart that Your plans are for my good—I just
need to follow You. I trust You with my life and
wait on the unfolding of each day's events as
You have ordered. My today, tomorrow, and
all the rest to come are in Your hands, so I am
able to live forward with full assurance and
continual hope that all will be well.

AMEN.

HOPE GIVES COURAGE

Since, then, we have such a hope,
we act with great boldness.
II CORINTHIANS 3:12

Father, knowing I am covered by Your grace
and free from the weight of sin helps me
to live with abandon. Knowing that even
when I misstep—because I will—I am free
of condemnation. This lifts the weight that
performance-centered living brings. My
hope for spending eternity with You shines
brighter than ever and instills the courage I
need for carrying out Your purpose for my
life—mistakes and all. Help me to extend
the same grace toward others so that they,
too, can know the freedom that hope
in You brings.
AMEN.

HOPE THAT'S SOUND

I [David] saw the Lord ever before me;
because He is at my right hand,
I will not be shaken. Therefore my heart is
glad and my tongue rejoices. Moreover,
my flesh will rest in hope.

ACTS 2:25-27

Father, because of the lasting hope that
comes from You, I am able to rest in Your
glory. I am sound and secure within, no
matter what swirls around me on the
outside. Through hope in You, I'm able to
have joy, lasting joy, and for this I lift my
praise to You. Thank You for the gift of rest
and peace through Jesus—the One who
doesn't change. In His name I pray.

AMEN.

HOPE FOR STRENGTH

Godliness is beneficial in every way,
since it holds promise for the present life
and also for the life to come....
For this reason we labor and strive, because
we have put our hope in the living God,
who is the Savior of all people.

I TIMOTHY 4:8, 10

Lord, I confess it's hard to be godly in every
way. The enemy knows just where my hot
buttons are, and he presses them every
day. But I try. I do not give up. I call to You
today and every day for help to do what's
right at all times. I look to You and hope in
You for the strength I need for today, with
assurance I'll have it again tomorrow and
the next—because You are faithful.
All glory to You.
AMEN.

THE HOPE OF SALVATION

Now may our Lord Jesus Christ Himself...
who has loved us and given us everlasting
comfort and encouragement and the
good [well-founded] hope [of salvation]...
encourage and strengthen your hearts.

II THESSALONIANS 2:16-17 AMP

Father, I love having hope in You because
when I do, my stance is grounded and will
not be swayed by the constant forces that
try to shake my faith. By Your hope, I live
secure in a glorious future ahead. I am
comforted and encouraged for pressing on
in the purpose and plan You have for me,
no matter what I face. You are with me and
will never leave. All praise be to You.

AMEN.

HOPE FOR ETERNAL LIFE

Yet I call this to mind, and therefore I have hope: Because of the LORD's faithful love we do not perish, for His mercies never end.

LAMENTATIONS 3:21-22

Lord, You are so faithful in Your love for me. I know there are times I've not been a very lovable person, yet You remain and show Your healing mercy. You understand and are quick to forgive and remind me that I always have hope for a new day and a fresh start with You. Thank You from my heart for renewed hope and strength to claim as my own. In Your loving kindness I pray.

AMEN.

THE RIGHT HOPE

Can any of the worthless foreign gods send
us rain? Does it fall from the sky by itself?
No.... Only You can do such things.
JEREMIAH 14:22 NLT

O Lord, I am tired, and I know it's because
I've been hoping in the wrong things.
A steady job, knowing the right people,
an impressive resume, having a full bank
account...I know these are all good, but to
put my hope in them is futile—they can all
be gone tomorrow and don't bring true rest
for my soul. Please forgive me and help me
start again. Today, I fix my gaze on You and
the promises You've given. You are the one
true hope for today and the future ahead.
In Christ's name.
AMEN.

HOPE THAT WON'T END

Do not long for what sinners have. But
always show great respect for the Lord.
There really is hope for you in days to
come. So your hope will not be cut off.
PROVERBS 23:17-18 NIRV

Father, it's so hard not to compare and see
how my neighbor, who doesn't care about
You, thrives and prospers at every turn.
First, help me to be content with what I
have because I know that the world's view
of success is not the same as Yours. Then,
help me remember that at any moment, her
prosperity could vanish, and she'd sink fast.
Help me be a light so that she might come
to know the source of hope—You.
All praise be to You.
AMEN.

HIS PROMISES FUEL HOPE

Such hope [in God's promises] never
disappoints us, because God's love has
been abundantly poured out within our
hearts through the Holy Spirit
who was given to us.

ROMANS 5:5 AMP

Lord, I love Your promises, because they
are true. They lead to the depths of Your
goodness and the freedom and grace that
are mine to claim. Thank You for the gift
of Your Holy Spirit in me, and for how You
instill a constant burning flame of hope no
matter how bleak a circumstance may look.
You are so faithful, and I am so glad to be
called Your child. In Jesus' name.

AMEN.

HIS LIGHT OF HOPE

Love finds no joy in unrighteousness but
rejoices in the truth. It bears all things,
believes all things, hopes all things,
endures all things.

I CORINTHIANS 13:6-7

Father, with so many falsehoods and
distractions clamoring around, I am grateful
to have Your truth to cling to. I'm grateful
for the joy You provide in the safety of Your
presence and the light of hope that shines
my way toward righteous living. Without
it, I'd be lost. Help me to endure through
hardship and rejoice daily so that, if nothing
else, Your truth will prevail. That's all that
matters. In Jesus' name.

AMEN.

SPIRIT OF HOPE

At that time you were without Christ,
excluded from the citizenship of Israel, and
foreigners to the covenants of promise,
without hope and without God in the world.

EPHESIANS 2:12

O Lord, thinking back on life before You
feels depressing. I worked and laughed
hard on the outside, but on the inside
I was downcast and without hope. You
transformed my life and brought true joy to
my present and my future. I love being part
of Your family and being called Your child.
Thank You for removing the separation I
had with You before and for sealing my life
with Your Spirit of hope. In Jesus' name.

AMEN.

HOPE FOR TOMORROW

If we have put our hope in Christ for this life only, we should be pitied more than anyone.

I CORINTHIANS 15:19

Lord, yes, I put my hope in You for today and tomorrow, but You give even more— You give hope for an eternal life with You. I am reminded that this life on earth does not end here. You keep Your home light burning, and it is a flame that will never go out. I can only imagine how wonderful a place it will be. What a loving God You are! All praise and glory to You.

AMEN.

JOYFUL IN HOPE

When you hope, be joyful. When you suffer,
be patient. When you pray, be faithful.
ROMANS 12:12 NIRV

Lord God, I will be joyful today because I
believe—I believe in You and that the hope
You give is real. When I dwell on this fact,
my heart swells with love and thanksgiving.
In hardship, You help me to endure. When
others disappoint, You prove Yourself
faithful time and again. And when I hope in
You, my heart fills with joy and anticipation
for the beauty that lies ahead. You are a
good God. This I pray in the holiness of
Your presence.

AMEN.

HOPE IS A CHOICE

I say, "The LORD is my portion, therefore I
will put my hope in Him."

LAMENTATIONS 3:24

O Lord, I can't count the times I have
needed Your mercy net to reach down
and catch me. They are too numerous.
Your faithfulness has been steadfast—You
have never failed me. I look to You today
in full hope that You are in my life, in my
circumstances, and in my heart to bring
assurance and peace that beats stronger
than any of my problems. Today is a new
day, and I will rejoice in knowing I am Yours.
In Jesus' name.

AMEN.

UNWAVERING HOPE

O my God, in You I [have unwavering]
trust [and I rely on You with steadfast
confidence], do not let me be ashamed or
my hope in You be disappointed.

PSALM 25:2 AMP

Heavenly Father, nothing and no one has
been as faithful in my life as You have been.
I call out to You day and night, and You
are there. I am comforted to know You are
with me always. You know my needs and
fill them. You love me when I'm not all that
lovable. You are the same faithful God to
me as You were to Moses, David, Paul, and
Jesus Himself. Therefore my hope remains
in You, my Rock and my Fortress.

AMEN.

CONFIDENT HOPE

For we have heard of your faith in Christ
Jesus and your love for all of God's people,
which come from your confident hope of
what God has reserved for you in heaven.

COLOSSIANS 1:4–5 NLT

Father, You are so very good. I not only
have confident hope for the future, I have
it for the present. That's because through
faith and the power of Your Spirit, I am
filled with more encouragement than I've
ever known. And it is my hope that Your
love will overflow onto others so they will
have the same love, the same confidence of
spending eternity with You.
By the power of Your Spirit.

AMEN.

SPREADING HOPE

We boast in God all day long;
we will praise Your name forever.

PSALM 44:8

Father, because of You I have hope that
doesn't wane. No matter how bleak things
may appear, I can hold on to You and know
all will be well. And it is my hope that as I
live out this day, I will be a vessel to spread
the good news about You to others without
thinking twice. You came to save the
world, not just me, so help my passion and
confidence flow out so that all I meet will
see You and see a light that draws them to
You. All praise to You forever.

AMEN.

HOPE IN JESUS' NAME

Look at My Servant. See My Chosen One.
He is My Beloved, in whom My soul delights.
I will put My Spirit upon Him.... His name
shall be the hope of all the world.

MATTHEW 12:18, 21 TLB

Jesus, You are the light and hope of the
world. Your name is above all names. I
rejoice with worship and praise for the
deep, lasting peace I have in my heart
because of You. Your name, Your sacrifice is
the never-ending hope of the world.
You alone are worthy.

AMEN.

HOPE FILLED

May the God of hope fill you with all joy
and peace in faith so that you overflow with
hope by the power of the Holy Spirit.
ROMANS 15:13 CEB

Lord, may my heart for You never run dry.
May nothing around me ever rob me of
the hope I have in You. No matter how
difficult a challenge, no matter the duration
of a trial, may my hope light keep burning
strong and Your glory be revealed. Now
I claim the joy and peace that are mine
through the power of Your Spirit. I want You
to reign in this day no matter what it brings.
AMEN.

APRIL

PEACE

BLESSED PEACE

The LORD gives His people strength;
the LORD blesses His people with peace.

PSALM 29:11

Lord, this is so true. Whenever I'm weak
and afraid and I call on You, You fill me with
peace like no other. You supply me with
strength and courage to walk through each
day's demands with hope in my heart. You
remind me that I am not alone—You're my
advocate at my every turn. The sound of
Your name hushes all other noise so that all
I can hear is Your breath of life in me. Thank
You for the blessing of Your peace.
In Jesus' name.

AMEN.

THE ANTIDOTE TO WORRY

Don't worry about anything, but in everything, through prayer and petition with thanksgiving, present your requests to God. And the peace of God, which surpasses all understanding, will guard your hearts and minds in Christ Jesus.

PHILIPPIANS 4:6–7

Father, I confess I often struggle with worry. So I turn to You now and release my needs to You and trust that You are in control and will provide. I pray that Your peace will overflow into my heart and that it will guard my mind from the enemy's attempt to take my mind off You. Today I will abide in Your lovingkindness and faithfulness toward me and have a heart full of thanksgiving and praise. To You I lift my prayers of love.

AMEN.

BE A PEACEMAKER

Watch the blameless and
observe the upright, for the person
of peace will have a future.
PSALM 37:37

Lord, I need Your peace. Not only to help
me stay calm in the face of the demands
and deadlines of each day, but so I can be
a person of peace to a broken world. So
many forces stir up conflict and hatred, but
I want to be Your influence to those around
me with gentleness and calm. Help me to
slow down and be a vessel of peace to lead
the lost to hope and a future with You.
In Jesus' precious name.
AMEN.

PATHWAY TO PEACE

Stand, therefore, with truth like a belt around your waist, righteousness like armor on your chest, and your feet sandaled with readiness for the gospel of peace.

EPHESIANS 6:14–15

Father, help me to remember that as I try to be a witness for You and share the truth of Your gospel, the enemy will resist. Clothe me with Your armor and let me not be discouraged but rather grow stronger in faith as I share about Your love and sacrifice with a lost world. Give me a willing heart to go wherever You lead and to be a testimony of the peace that can only come from You. In Christ's name I pray.

AMEN.

PEACEFUL SLEEP

I will both lie down and sleep in peace,
for you alone, LORD, make me live in safety.
PSALM 4:8

Lord, the world is so chaotic and at war on
many levels. If not for You, I'd be a wreck,
turning to the right and to the left in utter
fear. But You—the Prince of Peace—reach
down and bless me with indescribable calm.
For this I am so grateful. My soul is blessed
with sound sleep at night and refreshment
for each new day. That's because I am in
Your hands. You carry me and guard me
from disaster at all turns.
I lift my heart in praise to You.
AMEN.

HIS SACRIFICE
FOR MY PEACE

He was wounded and bruised for our sins.
He was beaten that we might have peace;
He was lashed—and we were healed!
ISAIAH 53:5 TLB

Jesus, it's sobering to think of what You
endured so that I could have lasting peace
and life. I am so very grateful for Your
sacrifice and humbled that You love me so
much. Forgive me for the times I take the
peace and healing You offer for granted. I
love You and worship Your holy presence in
this day and every day to come.
To You be all glory.
AMEN.

SECURE IN HIS PEACE

God is not a God of disorder but of peace.

I CORINTHIANS 14:33

Father, I ask that You protect my home—
surround the walls and guard it from evil.
May Your presence flow throughout each
room and fill them with a spirit of peace—a
peace that flows into the spirits of all who
enter. I pray that my family and friends
will sense that You are near, and may they
feel secure and at ease within their hearts.
Help me to be a conduit of Your love in
my speech and actions and, most of all,
my living testimony in the dailiness of life.
Thank You for hearing my prayer.

AMEN.

STANDING FOR PEACE

I have dwelt too long with those who hate
peace. I am for peace; but when I speak,
they are for war.

PSALM 120:6-7

Lord, there is so much hatred and meanness
in the air throughout this world. It is difficult
to speak my beliefs without igniting an
argument or controversy. Please protect
me from the opposing forces I face through
hateful headlines and Facebook posts.
Help me not to get caught up in having to
be right or respond to vile comments that
create more division. Instead, help peace
be at the core of my heart. Or give me the
strength to stay silent altogether. Help me
to stand firm in Your truth with gentleness.
In Christ's name I pray.

AMEN.

ABIDING PEACE

The way of the LORD is
a stronghold to the upright.
PROVERBS 10:29 AMP

Father, it seems as though every day
holds undercurrents that try to throw me
off balance and confuse the direction I'm
going. It's so easy to get off the course You
have set for me, but that's where I want to
be—in Your hands. Thank goodness You are
a force stronger than any other. You are a
refuge and tower of strength. Abiding at
the center of Your will is a wellspring of
comfort and peace for me to rest.
And I am so grateful.
AMEN.

WHEN THERE ISN'T PEACE

I did not come to bring peace....
I came to turn a man against his father,
a daughter against her mother, a daughter-
in-law against her mother-in-law;
and a man's enemies will be the members
of his household.

MATTHEW 10:34-36

Wow, Lord, this verse really hits at the
heart, but it's true. Professing my faith in
You has changed me, and change brings
conflict at times, especially within my
family. Help me to remember to live, act,
and speak in love. Help me remember that
You didn't come to bring peace, but that
You are peace itself. Only through knowing
You can there be true reconciliation
between the divides of different faiths. I'm
so glad to have You in my heart, Lord.

AMEN.

PROMOTE PEACE

Those who promote peace have joy.
PROVERBS 12:20 NET

Father, I know that at the beginning of
each new day, I have a choice about my
attitude—whether I'll grumble and stir up
strife or be grateful and promote peace.
Today I choose joy. I choose thanksgiving. I
choose forgiveness and peace toward those
who have hurt me. I am blessed beyond
measure, and I want others to know of Your
goodness as well. Give me eyes to see that
each person I encounter needs a touch
of Your love. Give me the courage and
determination to extend it. I want Your joy,
yes, but I want others to have it too and for
You to be glorified. In Jesus' name.

AMEN.

PERFECT PEACE

You will keep him in perfect peace,
whose mind is stayed on You,
because he trusts in You.

ISAIAH 26:3 NKJV

Father, sometimes I wake at early hours of
the morning and realize my mind is racing
over all my worries—and I feel frozen and
stressed. But then I remember that You are
there, waiting for me to turn my thoughts
toward You. And oh, what peace You bring
when I do. I trust in You alone and know
that You are watching over every detail and
orchestrating the fulfillment of every need.
Thank You for Your faithful love toward me.
I rest in Your care. In Jesus' name.

AMEN.

RIGHTEOUSNESS AND PEACE

The result of righteousness will be peace;
the effect of righteousness
will be quiet confidence forever.

ISAIAH 32:17

Father, I have noticed that when I do as
You say and follow Your lead, I have a quiet
confidence—as though no matter what
happens around me, I am in good hands
that protect and provide. I have found no
other source that gives this secure and
calming effect. And I know that when I
don't have peace, I am to stay away, even
run. I long for a quiet place to let my spirit
rest amid my busyness; I pray for peace
that overshadows the enormity of life's
demands. In You, I know I have both.
All praise in Jesus' name.

AMEN.

STRIVE TO BE AT PEACE

Have salt among yourselves,
and be at peace with one another.
MARK 9:50

Lord, I know that the only way to be at
peace with others is to walk with a humble
heart and speak with words that edify Your
truth. That means to season them with Your
blessing before they ever leave my mouth.
It means to lace my thoughts and words
with love and deliver them with a spirit of
gentleness. It means to clothe myself with
humility before I walk out my front door.
Help me to have this mindset every day so
that peace may rule and You are glorified.
In Jesus' name.
AMEN.

THINK ON HIM FOR PEACE

For the mind set on the flesh is death, but
the mind set on the Spirit is life and peace.

ROMANS 8:6 NASB

Lord, I know my thoughts are on the wrong
things when I lack peace. But there are
so many things that pull my focus from
You. From ads that pop up online, to
commercials on TV telling me to buy the
latest gadget, to problems robbing me of
joy—it's a daily battle. But I am determined
to keep my eyes on You today, not on
things I want or difficulties I face. I breathe
in Your spirit of peace and exhale out all the
other garbage that competes with You.
I pray with the fullness of my heart.

AMEN.

THE GIFT OF PEACE

The disciples were still talking about
[Jesus' resurrection] when Jesus Himself
suddenly stood among them.
He said, "May you have peace!"
LUKE 24:36 NIRV

Jesus, I believe that by the power of Your
Spirit You are with me now. Your presence
is evident because of the peace that I
carry in my heart. It's no less than a sweet
gift that I gladly receive and will embrace
throughout this day. Please stay with me,
walk with me, guide my steps, and steer
my thoughts to be captive to You and Your
goodness in my life. I trust in You and
thank You for Your presence.
I pray in the glory of Your name.
AMEN.

THE FULFILLMENT OF PEACE

Peace I leave with you. My peace I give to you. I do not give to you as the world gives. Don't let your heart be troubled or fearful.

JOHN 14:27

Jesus, it seems that everywhere I turn, society tries to lure my heart to latch onto what it says will bring peace. Accomplishments, acquiring things, living large, having fun...The media promotes living the good life, but none of it truly fills or lasts. Help me to see through the false promises and stay focused on being in Your presence and following Your will for my life. You promise peace, and You fulfill it every time I turn to You. Thank You for being true to Your word. With thanksgiving and praise.

AMEN.

PEACE IN SUFFERING

I have told you these things so that in Me
you may have peace. You will have suffering
in this world. Be courageous!
I have conquered the world.

JOHN 16:33

Lord, when You say we will have suffering
in this life, You were serious. There have
been obstacles and challenges greater
than I ever thought could happen. But You
say to be courageous, so I will. I am able,
knowing You are fighting my battles with
me. You are a shield of comfort and blanket
of peace for my heart. You keep me going
in the power of Your Spirit throughout each
day and into the night. Because of You, I
can be strong and at rest. All praise and
thanksgiving to You.

AMEN.

THE BOND OF PEACE

Live worthy of the calling you have
received, with all humility and gentleness,
with patience, bearing with one another in
love, making every effort to keep the unity
of the Spirit through the bond of peace.

EPHESIANS 4:1-3

Jesus, help me to live worthy of my
calling—I cannot do it alone. I get impatient
and tempted to do things my way instead
of Yours. By Your Spirit and power, help
my heart to remain humble and quick to
extend grace to others when they offend.
Help me to know when to have strong
boundaries and when to keep peace for the
sake of Your name. Help me to be a loving
influence to the lost around me so they
see You, which, I know, is at the core of my
testimony. I ask this in Your name.

AMEN.

PEACE AS A WAY OF LIFE

Work at living in peace with everyone,
and work at living a holy life.

HEBREWS 12:14 NLT

Father, forgive me. I often forget that my
life is not about me. And I get so caught
up in living and working, I forget about the
holiness and peace part. Make me ever so
sensitive to living at peace, especially with
so much division in our world. There is no
point in speaking my mind about anything
if there is no love and unity in the end.
Remind me that the reason for living is to
share the gospel of Your love with an angry
and broken people. I want the world
to see You.

AMEN.

WISDOM IN PEACE

The wisdom from above is first pure,
then peace-loving, gentle, compliant,
full of mercy and good fruits, unwavering,
without pretense.

JAMES 3:17

Father, oh how I love You and the
wisdom You provide. With so much false
information at the click of a mouse, I cling
to the richness and truths You breathe into
my life. Reading Your Word is the only thing
that satisfies my thirst for how to live a holy
and pleasing life. When I call on Your name
and share my heart with You, I am filled
with Your mercy and love to carry with me
each day in confidence and peace. You are
a wealth of treasure and I am grateful to be
Your child. All praise and glory to You.

AMEN.

PEACE IN DISCIPLINE

No discipline seems pleasant at the time,
but painful. Later...it produces a harvest of
righteousness and peace for those
who have been trained by it.

HEBREWS 12:11 NIV

Lord, this is so true—the peace that grows
and dwells after learning a hard lesson is
a tremendous gift. Help me to remember
this the next time I'm tempted to stray—
Your peace leaves, and it's an awful feeling.
Thank You for the serenity and calm that is
mine to claim as my constant companion
when I walk with You. It is a soothing balm
for my heart that I want to carry always.
In Jesus' name.
AMEN.

HOW TO LOVE LIFE

The one who wants to love life
and to see good days...Let him seek peace
and pursue it, because the eyes of the Lord
are on the righteous and
his ears are open to their prayer.

I PETER 3:10-12

Father, please do hear my prayer. I try
to seek and pursue peace, but I get so
distracted. There are people and problems
that take my gaze off You, and my heart
feels anything but at peace. But I seek You
now—the Prince of Peace. Guide me, help
me to walk in Your ways of truth and live
with pure motives for a good life and one
that is pleasing to You. In Jesus' name.

AMEN.

PEACE IN WAITING

My friends, while you are waiting, you
should make certain that the Lord finds you
pure, spotless, and living at peace.

II PETER 3:14 CEV

Lord, I can think of multiple times You've
found me as anything but pure, spotless,
and living at peace—and I'm so sorry. I
know what I ought to do but at times lack
the will to do it. Help me today to live in the
full expression of Your love as we all wait on
Your return. I claim Your new mercies and
the chance to be a pleasing aroma until that
time comes. Praise and glory to You.

AMEN.

PEACE-GIVING RESPONSES

A gentle answer turns away anger,
but a harsh word stirs up wrath.

PROVERBS 15:1

Father, I need Your help. Words can fly out
of my mouth before I even know I've said
them. I don't want to be just another hot
balloon that pops at someone I disagree
with. Put a guard over my mouth and
remind me to pause and pray before
reacting to hurtful or offensive words.
Convict me to want peace and love over
being right about something. Help me to
be gentle, even silent, when discussions
get heated, whether face to face or on
someone's online post. You are what
matters most, and more than anything,
I want to be an example of Your love.

AMEN.

PEACE IN CHANGE

There is an occasion for everything, and a
time for every activity under heaven.

ECCLESIASTES 3:1

Father, the seasons of life are ever
changing, and change always brings
unrest for my soul. The spring and summer
seasons are filled with happiness and
forward-moving goals. But the long nights
and cold days of fall and winter are much
more challenging. I want to walk in the
peace that You give through each change
in circumstances and surroundings as I
remember that You are over all—You are
very much in control. Help me be open to
the changes You want to work in me so
that I become mature and complete in Your
purposes for me. I trust in You.

AMEN.

ABUNDANT PEACE

Abundant peace belongs to those
who love your instruction;
nothing makes them stumble.

PSALM 119:165

Father God, I love Your Word and the
wisdom it contains. You state so clearly
how I am to live, and You shower me with
promises that bless my life—including
abundant peace. Confusion can rush in at
any given moment, but with You as my
anchor, I can rest assured and lean into the
promise of Your presence and guidance. I
trust in You and Your ways—I want to follow
Your lead. In Jesus' name I pray
with a grateful heart.

AMEN.

THE ENEMY OF PEACE

Regard Christ the Lord as holy, ready at any
time to give a defense to anyone who asks
you for a reason for the hope that is in you.
Yet do this with gentleness.

I PETER 3:15–16

Father, help me to remember that sharing
the gospel attracts the enemy's offense
so the lost will stay lost. And he does
this through arguments and quarreling
over Your words of truth. Help me to see
these tactics for what they are. Give me
a clear mind, a calm spirit, and gentle
responses. Help me not to get defensive
over questions or challenges but rather be
confident in a way that promotes peace
and, most of all, Your love.
All glory be to You.

AMEN.

PEACEFUL PURSUIT

Let us pursue what promotes peace
and what builds up one another.

ROMANS 14:19

Lord, I confess I have a critical spirit that
quietly resides deep down, and when I
notice a fault in someone else, it raises its
ugly head. But I know it's not of You. And
I know that my own pride is what feeds it.
Please humble my heart today and strip
away the power of its presence. Help me
to see good in and promote love on others
to bring unity and peace. Give me words
to encourage and lift up my sisters and
brothers so that, together, our glad hearts
can receive the fullness of Your joy.
In Christ I pray.

AMEN.

PEACE IN REJOICING

Rejoice, set things right, be encouraged,
agree with one another, live in peace, and
the God of love and peace will be with you.
II CORINTHIANS 13:11 NET

Lord, I notice the first word in this verse is
rejoice—before all else, I must rejoice and
be glad. So I do that now. You have made
this new day, and I lift up my praise and
thanksgiving for Your mighty acts of love
and faithfulness. I am full of Your blessing;
Your calming presence abounds. Your Spirit
in me brings encouragement, steadiness,
and peace, for which I am so thankful.
In Jesus' name.
AMEN.

MAY

TRUST

TRUST IN THE LORD

Trust in the Lord with all your heart,
and do not rely on your own understanding;
in all your ways know Him,
and He will make your paths straight.

PROVERBS 3:5-6

Father, it's hard to turn off my thoughts
about how to work through problems I'm
facing. I know I need to find solutions, yet I
must leave room for trusting in You. I know
my intellect can only think so far and it can
be deceiving. At some point I must release
the unknowns to You and trust You with all
my heart that You'll show me step by step
what to do and when. I cast my cares on
You now and entrust them to You
with all my heart.

AMEN.

A HEART THAT BELIEVES

The LORD said to Moses...
"How long will they not believe in Me,
despite all the [miraculous] signs which I
have performed among them?"
NUMBERS 14:11 AMP

O Lord, I confess I am guilty of this same
thing—not trusting in You after You've
clearly worked wonders in my life. You'd
think that because of the goodness You
have displayed toward me, I wouldn't
hesitate at all to trust in You when
circumstances around me are unclear.
Please forgive me and help me now to ward
off any doubt that comes to mind. You
have been faithful before, and I believe You
will continue to bless and provide in Your
perfect way and time. In Jesus' name.
AMEN.

BE A LOYAL FOLLOWER

Your loyal followers trust in You, for You,
LORD, do not abandon those
who seek Your help.

PSALM 9:10 NET

Father, this is so true. Since following You,
I cannot think of a time You ever left me
on my own. But I can think of times I've
abandoned You in order to follow my own
heart—and I live with the regret. But I am
stayed on You now. I trust You with my
life and how You want to use it. Please
continue to help and guide me, and give me
courage to go where You lead. I trust You
completely now as the saints of old trusted
You thousands of years ago. I pray in the
presence of Jesus.

AMEN.

TRUST IS THE ONLY ANSWER

In spite of this you did not trust the LORD your God, who went before you on the journey to seek out a place for you to camp.

DEUTERONOMY 1:32-33

O Lord, this is so convicting because I do the same thing: in spite all the ways You've provided and blessed my life, I still lack trust. Please forgive me. My focus on my problems overshadows my focus on Your faithfulness, and I'm sorry. I look to You now and remember...I remember the kindness You have shown and the answers to prayers—sometimes even greater than I ever thought possible. You are a good, good God, and I love You.

AMEN.

FRAGILE TRUST

His source of confidence is fragile; what he trusts in is a spider's web. He leans on his web, but it doesn't stand firm. He grabs it, but it does not hold up.

JOB 8:14–15

Father, I shudder to think of all the things this world tells me to put my trust in, especially my own judgment. I work hard at creating my own agenda based on my reason and logic, and yet, as You say, it is fragile. I want to be on solid ground and find success and favor in the days, months, and years ahead, so I turn to You and place my trust in You. I rest in indescribable peace knowing You are at the helm of my life. In Jesus' name.

AMEN.

TRUST IN HIS STRENGTH

But those who trust in the Lᴏʀᴅ will find
new strength. They will soar high on wings
like eagles. They will run and not grow
weary. They will walk and not faint.
ISAIAH 40:31 NLT

Father, sometimes life can be so exhausting
and overwhelming, I continuously return
to the humble state that I cannot bear
the weight and pressure alone. You
have been a constant source of strength
and refreshment as I place my full and
committed trust in You for help. I believe in
my heart that You won't give me more than
I can handle and that You will provide new
power and vigor to overcome any weakness
or temptation to give up. In Your great and
glorious name I pray.
AMEN.

TRUST HIS WORD

The instruction of the Lord is perfect,
renewing one's life; the testimony of
the Lord is trustworthy, making the
inexperienced wise.

PSALM 19:7

Lord, I believe Your Word is truth. Each
story You tell, each pledge of assurance
breathes new life in me in ways I cannot
explain except that You are present, You
are there in the pages calling me to You.
The knowledge I gain through the chapters
is priceless, as are the stories of faith that
inspire and help me to know how to live.
Your faithfulness reads through centuries
of promises fulfilled, including that of a
Savior—the One who died on my behalf so
I can spend eternity with You. All praise be
to You, Father God.

AMEN.

COMPLETE TRUST

Immediately the father cried out, "I do
believe! Help me to believe more!"
MARK 9:24 NCV

Father, oh how I can relate to this man's
struggle with unbelief. I want to believe in
You to the point that there is no hesitation
on my part when it comes to trusting You
with my life. I know the only way this will
happen is if I acknowledge any area that
I don't wholly trust You with. Please show
me what I'm holding on to, what I am still
trying to control myself. I want to release it
to You so my trust in You is complete. The
way a toddler trustingly jumps to her father
in a pool, I want the same pure and simple
belief that You will catch me every day that
I walk in faith in You. In Jesus' name.
AMEN.

NOTHING TO FEAR

Behold, God is my salvation; I will trust,
and will not be afraid; for the Lord God
is my strength and my song, and he has
become my salvation.

ISAIAH 12:2 ESV

Lord, You are my salvation and my hope at
all times. You've delivered a way—through
Your Son, Jesus—for me to enter into Your
presence of grace, now and for eternity.
The weight and burden of my sins are lifted,
and I can sing a new song of love to You.
Because of Your faithfulness, I can trust in
You with my whole heart and being. I have
nothing to fear on this earth—
You are sovereign and over all.
All praise and glory to You.

AMEN.

DEPEND ON HIM ONLY

You will keep the mind that is
dependent on You in perfect peace,
for it is trusting in You.

ISAIAH 26:3

Lord, when I focus on my circumstances
and trust in the limits of my imagination,
I become anxious and stressed. But each
time I turn my thoughts to You and the
love You have for me, I am at peace. I can't
help but trust You fully because You fill my
heart with hope and my body with peace
and rest. No one and no thing can compare
to the greatness of You, so in You my trust
will lie. Thank You for being my refuge and
constant source of strength. In Jesus' name.

AMEN.

FLOURISHING TRUST

Anyone trusting in his riches will fall,
but the righteous will flourish like foliage.
PROVERBS 11:28

Father, society says a full bank account, a
fancy car, a beautiful home, and status in
my community will mean a full and stable
life. But it's all a lie from an enemy who
doesn't want anyone to be truly secure.
Knowing You, living for You, carrying out
Your purposes, walking and being led by
Your Spirit—this is where my trust will
remain because You promise to complete
what You have started in my life. I love and
trust You today, tomorrow, and always.
All glory to You.
AMEN.

STOP TRUSTING YOURSELF

In fact, we felt sure that we were going
to die. But this made us stop trusting in
ourselves and start trusting God,
who raises the dead to life.

II CORINTHIANS 1:9 CEV

Father, because Jesus sacrificed Himself
on my behalf, I am sealed with the promise
of spending eternity with You. This means
I no longer have to fear death—I can trust
You for eternal life. What relief and joy this
brings! I no longer walk in fear because my
very life is in Your hands. I am filled with
the confidence of Your presence and power,
knowing my future is secure. Thank You,
Jesus, for Your gift of sacrifice.

AMEN.

TRUST IN GOD'S WISDOM

A man is a fool to trust himself! But those
who use God's wisdom are safe.

PROVERBS 28:26 TLB

Lord, not only do I not trust myself, I ask
that You save me from myself! I am my
own worst enemy and shudder to think of
the times I thought I knew the answers to
my problems, only to find I made bigger
messes in the end. I look to You from this
day forward and commit to trusting Your
ways, Your resources, Your promises, and
Your power in me. You lead and guide in
ways I don't always understand, but I trust
that You have only my best interest and
Your great glory in mind. With sincere
and full devotion.

AMEN.

TRUST IN HIS DELIVERANCE

When Daniel was brought up from the den,
he was found to be unharmed,
for he trusted in his God.

DANIEL 6:23

Father, if Daniel can trust You to deliver
him from a den of hungry lions, I know
I can trust You to be with me in the
circumstances I face today. But even more,
I trust You no matter how things turn out.
I can't see past the immediate details of
what I face, but You see the bigger overall
picture, and You know how best to arrange
and to act so that Your presence is evident
to all who are watching. I trust You to lead,
guide, and deliver me so that You will
receive glory and I will receive blessing.

AMEN.

TRUST IN HIS PROTECTION

The fear of mankind is a snare, but the one
who trusts in the Lord is protected.

PROVERBS 29:25

Lord God, You are the God of truth. You do
not deceive or mislead the way people so
often do. I look to You today for help as I
work through today's challenges. Let Your
Spirit guide me while I rest in the safety of
Your hands. Give me strength to wait on
You and Your perfect timing before each
step and courage to move when You say
it's time to move. Help me to weigh outside
counsel with the filter of Your Word and the
protection of Your presence. I trust in You,
my loving and faithful God.
All praise be to You.

AMEN.

TRUST HIS SAVING GRACE

This saying is trustworthy and deserving of
full acceptance: "Christ Jesus came into the
world to save sinners."

I TIMOTHY 1:15

O Lord, my heart is filled with sweet relief
to know that You came to save—You came
to save me! Your mercies are new every
morning, and Your faithfulness is great. I
believe and embrace Your sacrifice and
soak in this moment of joy overflowing for
such a great gift. Thank You for saving me,
for saving humankind—there is no greater
love than this. You proved Your love for us
all through Your death, therefore, how can I
not trust You completely with my life?
In Your precious name I pray.

AMEN.

TRUST IN TRUE LIFE

This saying is trustworthy: For if we died
with Him, we will also live with Him.

II TIMOTHY 2:11

Father, the enemy is cunning and deceptive
at making my "self" look great on the
throne of my life. But I want to see through
the lies and ask Your heart to take supreme
residence in mine. I want to live for You and
be used to complete Your purposes for me
in the overall plan of Your kingdom. I would
rather spend one day in Your courts and
experience true fullness of life than spend
a thousand elsewhere. As I die to my own
selfish ways, I trust in the newness of life
that You give. All glory to You,
my loving Savior.

AMEN.

TRUST IN HIS PROMISES

All Scripture is God-breathed
and is useful for teaching...and training
in righteousness, so that the servant of God
may be thoroughly equipped
for every good work.

II TIMOTHY 3:16-17 NIV

Father, the gift of Your Word is the finest
of treasures and greatest of sources for
arming myself with wisdom and truth in a
chaotic world. Every word can be trusted
for helping; every story can be used as a
means of inspiration for spurring me on
with courage and resolve that You are
with me. Most of all, I love hearing from
Your heart about how to live so that I can
experience the greatest communion and
blessing with You each moment of the day.
In Your holy name.

AMEN.

THE VOICE OF TRUTH

While [Peter] was still speaking...
a voice from the cloud said:
"This is My beloved Son, with whom I am
well-pleased. Listen to Him!"

MATTHEW 17:5

Jesus, so many voices clamor for my
attention, I get confused about which one
to listen to. All I can do is stop and call
out to You to quiet the sounds and calm
my nerves. I want to hear Your voice—it's
the only one I know I can trust to speak
truth into my heart. You are the way, the
truth, and the life that I want to follow and
emulate. Please drown out all other noises
so that I can hear Your voice perfectly clear.
All thanks and praise to You.

AMEN.

GUARD YOUR HEART

Guard your heart above all else,
for it is the source of life.
PROVERBS 4:23

Dear Lord, trusting in You means freedom
for my soul. It creates a seal of armor
around my heart that keeps me from harm
and lets me dance in the protection of
Your presence. Please ward off the enemy's
attempts to injure my heart and instill
negative thoughts in my mind. Instead,
guard them both with Your coat of love
and life. I want to live and run freely in full
and complete trust in You, and I know I can
when You are watching over me. Thank You
for Your shelter and care.
In Jesus' sweet name.
AMEN.

TRUST IN HIS FAITHFULNESS

I have trusted in Your faithful love; my heart
will rejoice in Your deliverance.
I will sing to the LORD because He has
treated me generously.

PSALM 13:5-6

Father, You have blessed my life so
abundantly; You have surrounded me
with favor in more ways than I can count.
When I think on times You've delivered me
from the messes I've made, the falls I've
encountered—each time You were there to
pick me up and cover me with Your grace.
You have poured out to me the promises
of Your Word and Your faithfulness to fulfill
them. I am ever so grateful for Your love—
a love I trust to sustain my very life.

AMEN.

TRUST THAT SAFEGUARDS

You are my rock and my fortress;
You lead and guide me for Your name's
sake. You will free me from the net
that is secretly set for me.

PSALM 31:3-4

Father, each moment throughout my day,
the enemy tries to get my focus off You
and cause me stress over the demands I'm
facing. Please safeguard my attention to
keep You at the center of everything—my
words, my thoughts, my work, and my
actions. I claim the confidence that is mine
when I look to You as my Rock of life, and I
trust in the secure foundation You provide.
Bless this day to be without wavering or
second guessing as I keep my eyes
fixed on You.

AMEN.

TRUST IN HIS PROVISION

He waters the mountains from His palace....
He causes grass to grow for the livestock
and provides crops for man to cultivate...
and bread that sustains human hearts.

PSALM 104:13-15

Father, Your provision is all around—it is
abundant beyond what I deserve. You've
provided in the past, and I trust You will
meet my needs now. Help me not to dwell
on tomorrow. I know You'll be there loving
Your way into everything I face. Your
faithfulness has been evident since the
beginning of time, and it is obvious now. I
trust You for Your provision today and the
next day. All thanks be to Jesus.

AMEN.

TRUST HIS LEADING

Test me, Lord, and try me; examine my
heart and mind. For Your faithful love
guides me, and I live by Your truth.
PSALM 26:2-3

Father, please do examine my heart and
let me know if there is anything—thought,
word, or attitude—that is offensive to You.
The enemy is so subtle at fooling me into
doing things that seem okay yet are not
quite in line with Your Word. I want to be
sensitive to Your leading and the nudges
You give when I've said or done something
that isn't in harmony with Your ways. I want
to trust in Your faithful love alone.
AMEN.

TRUST IN HIS WAYS

I constantly trust in the LORD; because He is
at my right hand, I will not be upended.

PSALM 16:8 NET

Lord, I cannot count the number of nights
I've spent lying awake thinking on the past
day's events. I wonder how I could have
responded to challenges differently for
better outcomes. But then I remember that
all I can do is learn from my mistakes and
continue to trust Your ways, not my own.
Knowing You are with me and in control of
all things calms my spirit and blesses me
with peace like no other, and I am thankful.
In Jesus' name.

AMEN.

TRUST HIM WHEN YOU TITHE

"Bring the full tenth into
the storehouse.... Test Me in this way,"
says the LORD of Armies.

MALACHI 3:10

Father, when it comes to tithing, I feel
nervous—I worry I won't have enough left
to pay my bills. Ten percent is a lot, yet
Your Word says to return that much back
to You. It even says to test You to see if You
will not bless and provide in abundance. It
does feel convicting not to trust You in this
when You have been so faithful in my life.
So I will trust You now and step out in faith,
believing that You will provide when I tithe.
In Jesus' name.

AMEN.

TRUST HIS WAYS

For My thoughts are not your thoughts,
and your ways are not My ways.

ISAIAH 55:8

Lord, I get confused when I think I should
do one thing yet You lead me to do
something that doesn't make sense. These
are the times when I have to choose whom
I am going to serve—You or myself. I guess
it boils down to whether or not I trust You
enough with the outcome and believe it
will be for my best interest and for Your
glory. Please forgive my hesitation at times.
My life is not my own—Your goodness and
splendor are the goal. In Your name
I place my trust.

AMEN.

TRUST THAT HE SEES

Do not fret (whine, agonize) because of him
who prospers in his way, because of the
man who carries out wicked schemes.

PSALM 37:7 AMP

Father, it's hard to watch someone who is
arrogant and doesn't serve You prosper
in whatever they do, while I seem to
be overlooked. Help me to believe with
confidence that You see all things, and You
know the intent of everyone's hearts—and
that my reward will come in its time. You
are in control, and I am right where You
want me. Help me not to compare my life
with another's but learn to have patience as
I draw from the peace You put in my heart.
All praise and glory to Your name.

AMEN.

TRUST HIM TO VICTORY

The Rock—His work is perfect; all His ways
are just. A faithful God...He is righteous
and true.

DEUTERONOMY 32:4

Father, I'm in a trial that is testing my faith,
and the enemy keeps whispering for me to
give up. But I love You and know You love
me. I have to believe You are with Me now
and orchestrating events that will work for
my good in the end. I trust You to guide my
steps and lead me to victory, no matter how
thick the battle gets. I trust You to protect
my heart and guard my thoughts so that
Your strength and power will rule in the
end. In the power of Jesus in me I pray.

AMEN.

TRUST HIM WITH FUTURE GENERATIONS

Start a youth out on his way; even when he
grows old he will not depart from it.

PROVERBS 22:6

Lord, I think of our youth today and how
so many who've grown up in church don't
stay in church after they've left home. I pray
Your voice will always call to them: that the
longings of this world will not satisfy but
leave them empty and wanting more of
You. I entrust them to You to have Your way
so that their eyes would be enlightened
to Your truth over the lies and false
testimonies that lure them away from Your
house. Help them to see that trust in You is
the only way toward life and fulfillment.

In Jesus' name.

AMEN.

TRUST HIM TO THE FINISH LINE

Let us run with endurance the race that lies before us, keeping our eyes on Jesus, the source and perfecter of our faith.

HEBREWS 12:1-2

Father, this race of life on this earth is hard. I pray for the endurance I need to keep going with honor and integrity, and I look to You to see me through to the finish line. You are my God, my Rock, and my Stronghold—in You and only You do I place my trust. Direct my path and clear the way for Your kingdom to grow and flourish with lives that come to know Your truth and Your saving grace. I pray this in Jesus' name.

AMEN.

JUNE

JOY

THE RADIANCE OF JOY

Those who look to him are radiant with joy.

PSALM 34:5

Lord, this is true. I have seen people who
love You with a glow and presence that
radiate with joy—it is unmistakable and
luring. It is a living testimony to the life You
give and the hope You instill deep within
the soul. Without You and the joy that
You bring, life has no meaning. Help me to
realize the heavenly purpose that reigns
here on earth and to walk by Your Spirit of
joy in a way that others take notice of and
want for themselves. In Your sweet name.

AMEN.

THE TRUE SOURCE OF JOY

Then I will go to Your altar, O God;
You are the source of my happiness.

PSALM 43:4 GNT

Father, forgive me for all the times I look
to things and activities to fill my heart
with satisfaction and joy instead of simply
spending time with You. I know those other
things aren't bad, but they are empty unless
You are the main focus of worship and very
breath of life. I love You and thank You for
filling all my cracks of need with peace,
happiness, and Your faithful presence.
In Jesus' name.

AMEN.

TEST MY HEART

Deceit fills hearts that are plotting for evil;
joy fills hearts that are planning for good!
PROVERBS 12:20 TLB

Lord, test my heart and show me any way
that my actions—and the motives behind
them—are insincere or self-seeking toward
others. Help me to be more deliberate in
showing love and kindness because, when
I do, I always feel Your peace laced with a
thread of joy, and that is a great gift to me.
In Jesus' name and power I pray.

AMEN.

JOY IN NEW BIRTH

Because of His great mercy He has given us new birth into a living hope through the resurrection of Jesus Christ from the dead.

I PETER 1:3

Father, I'll never forget the day I came to know You as my personal Savior. I was literally reborn into a new life with new meaning. You gave me a new heart with a new start. No, my problems didn't go away, but I faced them with a new perspective and a new resolve. You have brought me joy I never thought I'd call my own, love I never thought I'd have, and a life I never dreamed could or would be possible. Thank You, Father, for Your great love.

AMEN.

JOY IN HARD DAYS

On a good day, enjoy yourself; on a
bad day, examine your conscience. God
arranges for both kinds of days so that we
won't take anything for granted.

ECCLESIASTES 7:14 THE MESSAGE

Lord, thank You for the days when joy leads
the way and overshadows every problem I
have. I consider them as customized gifts
planned just for me. Help me hold on to
joy during the hard days by remembering
that a loving and caring God is in control
of both, not just the good ones. You are an
anchor that holds me steady and secure,
and I am grateful. All praise to You.

AMEN.

JOY ON THE SABBATH

This is a sacred day before our Lord.
Don't be dejected and sad,
for the joy of the Lord is your strength!

NEHEMIAH 8:10 NLT

Father, the Sabbath—Your holy day—is
the best reason for looking away from my
hardships and devoting my attention wholly
unto You. Yes, it's an act of obedience, but
it is also a gift of rest and rejuvenation for
my soul. You have blessed my life in so
many ways, my heart is strengthened when
I recount the abundance You have poured
onto me. Thank You for being such a loving
and faithful God. In Jesus' name.

AMEN.

JOY IN FORGIVENESS

How joyful is the one whose transgression
is forgiven, whose sin is covered!

PSALM 32:1

O Lord, I am so humbled and thankful that
You are forgiving and gracious toward
me. The weight of my sin was heavy and
exhausting on my soul before I knew You,
but You cover me now with freedom and
new life. The burden I once felt has been
lifted and my guilt is gone. My heart is filled
with joy and praise for Your goodness and
for knowing I have a new, clean start today.
With thanksgiving and praise.

AMEN.

HE IS RISEN!

So [Mary Magdalene and Mary] left the
tomb quickly with fear and great joy, and
ran to tell [the good news to] the disciples.
MATTHEW 28:8 AMP

Jesus, what a rush of emotion and joy the
Marys must have felt when they found You
gone from the tomb! To see firsthand that
You had risen! It is the greatest miracle
to behold, and now Your Spirit lives on
in me. Thank You for Your sacrifice and
faithfulness to me and to the world of
followers who love and worship You.
Because You rose, we all can live!
In Your great name.
AMEN.

NEW SONGS OF JOY

Sing a new song to him; play skillfully on
the strings, with a joyful shout.

PSALM 33:3

Father, because of Your love and grace,
Your mercy and forgiveness, You put a
new song in my heart today. I am set free
from the weight of my sin, and my heart is
overflowing with love for You because of it.
I lift songs of praise and gladness and joy
for Your greatness and care. Thank You for
being so very good to me. In Jesus' name.

AMEN.

JOY IN OPPOSITION

Paul and Barnabas shook the dust off their
feet.... And the disciples were filled
with joy and the Holy Spirit.
ACTS 13:51-52

Lord, I love that I can have joy no matter
how harsh my surroundings. When I face
opposition or someone who is offensive, I
can shake off the ugly residue and let joy
fill my heart anyway. I want to remain lifted
by the clouds of gladness You well up in my
heart and pray it spreads onto others
so they will delight in You too.
In the power of Your love.
AMEN.

JOY IN REPENTANCE

There will be more joy in heaven
over one sinner who repents than over
ninety-nine righteous people who don't
need repentance.

LUKE 15:7

Father, it's a very emotional and wonderful
feeling to know You are present, attentively
listening, and waiting to heal every humble
heart that pours out words of confession
and love toward You. I rejoice with You in
heaven because it's literally a life-saving
experience. You give life and save life, and
that is the most precious celebration of all.
With songs of praise to You.

AMEN.

KINGDOM JOY

The kingdom of God is not eating and
drinking, but righteousness, peace, and joy.

ROMANS 14:17

Father, this is so true—what the world says
will bring satisfaction and happiness is the
opposite of what You say. No amount of
money, popularity, or fun living comes even
close to the lasting, deep contentment that
comes from abiding in You and spreading
Your love onto others. Be with me today
and help me remember this the next time
I'm tempted to do something that would be
outside of Your will for me. In Jesus' name.

AMEN.

FRUITFUL JOY

But the fruit of the Spirit is...joy.
GALATIANS 5:22

Lord, I can tell when I am walking closely
with You because those are the times I feel
the most secure and joyful in my heart. Help
me to stay close and not get distracted by
things or people who pull me away from
You. I want Your spirit in me to grow and
reflect Your presence to people around me
so there is no mistaking that I am Your child
and You are my great and almighty Father.
Praise to You, from whom all blessings flow.

AMEN.

JOY FOR OUR FINAL DESTINATION

He was willing to die a shameful death
on the cross because of the joy He knew
would be His afterwards.

HEBREWS 12:2 TLB

Jesus, it breaks my heart whenever I think
of the horrible and gruesome death You
endured on my behalf. There is no way for
me to repay You, yet You were still willing
to go to that cross. And because You did, I
rejoice from the rooftop that I am spending
eternity with You. Thank You! Thank You for
Your sacrifice and the gladness I am able to
experience because of it.
In Your sweet name I pray.
AMEN.

THE JOY OF THE LORD

His lord said to him, "Well done, good and
faithful servant; you were faithful over a
few things, I will make you ruler over many
things. Enter into the joy of your lord."

MATTHEW 25:21 NKJV

Father, because of You, I am doing things
I never thought possible. Devotion of life,
service on Your behalf, love extended to
the lost—whatever I do, I want to hear
the words "Well done, good and faithful
servant." The joy that is mine as I grow in
faith and responsibility is fulfilling beyond
measure. Thank You for Your faithfulness
and blessings. In Jesus' name.

AMEN.

BE JOY FOR OTHERS

A joyful heart makes a face cheerful, but a
sad heart produces a broken spirit.

PROVERBS 15:13

Father, when I see anyone with a downcast
expression, my heart feels heavy with
compassion. That's because I fear they
don't know You or have hope or purpose
for their life. Help me to be a ray of love and
sunshine for them. Help me to permeate
the blessing of Your presence onto them
so they know they've been touched by
something supernatural and want more.
Because of You, I'm able to truly smile and
reach out with sincerity of heart to others.
With thanksgiving and praise.

AMEN.

JOY FOR ALL

They have been tested by great troubles.
And they are very poor. But they gave
much because of their great joy.

II CORINTHIANS 8:2 ICB

Lord, Your presence in my life brings such
comfort and delight, especially in difficult
times. Your anchor of hope and gladness
of heart are far greater than any of my
problems. I trust in You, so I know I can
freely give to others in far greater need
than me, because I want them to hold the
promise of Your love and the fullness of
Your joy the way I do. Whatever it takes for
You to become real to someone in need, I
want to do it. In Jesus' name.

AMEN.

JOY IN FELLOWSHIP

Every day they devoted themselves to
meeting together in the temple, and broke
bread from house to house. They ate their
food with joyful and sincere hearts.

ACTS 2:46

Lord, fellowship with other believers is one
of the greatest joys I know. That's because
there's a time and chance to love on others
and be loved in return. Your love brings
healing to my heart and new energy to my
spirit, and sharing in the delight that You
bring is so special and lasting. Yes, eating
is always nice, but food for my soul is what
satisfies the most. With thanksgiving
and praise.

AMEN.

JOY IN TRIALS

Consider it a great joy...whenever
you experience various trials,
because you know that the testing of
your faith produces endurance.

JAMES 1:2-3

Father, it's hard to consider it a joy in
hardships and trials. But because Your
Word says to, I will. I trust You—to be in
control, to redeem anything that's lost,
and to grow me in ways You want so I can
be more powerful and effective for Your
kingdom. Knowing You're with me to guide
my steps and lead the way, I can rest in the
joy You bring, no matter the circumstances.
In Jesus' name.

AMEN.

JOY INCREASING

Walk worthy of the Lord...bearing fruit
in every good work and growing in the
knowledge of God, being strengthened with
all power, according to His glorious might.

COLOSSIANS 1:10-11

Lord, growing in Your knowledge,
increasing in strength and power, bringing
pleasure to You—knowing these are the
fruit of my efforts while serving You can't
help but bring tremendous joy to my heart.
You are a wellspring of abundance and the
source of all that is good. I want to share in
and be part of the inheritance that
You give. In Jesus' name.

AMEN.

JOY IN JUSTICE

How glad the nations will be, singing for
joy because you are their King and will give
true justice to their people!

PSALM 67:4 TLB

Father, I am so glad You are a God of
justice. You see all dishonest acts—You
know the heart of every person. It is hard
not to lash out at someone who's done
wrong to me, but I take rest in knowing You
will deal with them far better than I ever
could. Help me to claim the joy that is mine
from being sure You will act accordingly so
that righteousness will reign as it should.
I lift my heart to You.

AMEN.

HOLD ON TO JOY

You received our message with joy from the
Holy Spirit in spite of the trials and sorrows
it brought you.

I THESSALONIANS 1:6 TLB

Father, I love how, no matter how heavy and
thick my trial, I am able to remain secure
in the joy that You give. This is the day You
have made, and I choose to overcome what
I don't like about it with Your promises—
promises of hope, of love that will not end,
and of the contentment that comes from
joy through Your Spirit that lives in me.
Thank You for holding on to me as I hold on
to gladness in You.

AMEN.

GLORIOUS JOY

Though not seeing him now,
you believe in him, and you rejoice with
inexpressible and glorious joy.

I PETER 1:8

Father, I do believe, and I rejoice with a full
and grateful heart for Your Holy Spirit, who
is alive and working in me. I see evidence
of Your presence all around in the smallest
details of my very life. You surround me
with indescribable peace regardless of
what I am facing. I can't not lift my words
of praise to You and smile from within
knowing I am loved and cared for by
You, the Creator of the universe and the
heavens. In Jesus' wonderful name.

AMEN.

JOY IN HIS PRESENCE

Now to Him who is able to protect you
from stumbling and to make you stand in
the presence of His glory,
without blemish and with great joy.
JUDE 24

Lord, to stand in Your glory is almost
inconceivable for me to grasp, yet it's
true—as Your child, Your presence is
manifest in me. This brings great joy to
my heart considering where I came from
before knowing You. Help me always to
remember that You are with me, sharing
Your goodness while guarding my steps
and protecting my way.
In Your great name I pray.
AMEN.

JOY FOR TODAY

When I am filled with cares,
Your comfort brings me joy.

PSALM 94:19

O Father, You know the cares and concerns
on my heart today—and I'm so glad I can
bring them to You. Help me to do my part
in working through my struggles and then
release what I can't control into Your hands.
Please wrap Your comfort around me and
fill me with Your power and strength. Turn
my worries for tomorrow into joy for today
that cannot be broken. I love You so deeply
and pray in Your name.

AMEN.

LOST JOY

Joy has left our hearts;
our dancing has turned to mourning.
The crown has fallen from our head.
Woe to us, for we have sinned.
LAMENTATIONS 5:15–16

Father, I humble myself before You and
search my thoughts for any offensive
way in me. Please show me anything I do
that displeases You or any way I live that
hurts my testimony of Your gospel. I ask
for Your mercy and forgiveness, cleansing
and healing so that nothing will keep Your
peace and delight from dwelling in my
heart. I love You and pray this
in Jesus' name.
AMEN.

ROBED WITH JOY

The wilderness pastures overflow,
and the hills are robed with joy.
The pastures are clothed with flocks and
the valleys covered with grain.

PSALM 65:12-13

Father, I love to soak in the beauty of
Your creation. It enraptures my eyes with
the divine touch of Your handiwork. The
abundant life that roams, the bright and
colorful backdrops—it is all-encompassing
of how artistic and lovely You are. I want to
walk in the pleasure of Your company today
and soak in every ounce of the splendor
that surrounds my heart. All praise be to
You for such goodness.

AMEN.

JOY FROM HIS WORD

Your decrees are my heritage forever;
they are the joy of my heart.
PSALM 119:111 NRSV

Lord, I love Your Word—it is powerful and
alive. The commands, advice, and guidance
add security and comfort for my daily
living. But even more, I get to enter into
Your world and learn more about You—my
Savior and my Redeemer. And I love that
it won't change—it stands true for my
lifetime and for generations to follow until
You return. I know I can depend on the
permanence of Your ways for always. Thank
You for such a gift! In Jesus' name.
AMEN.

SECURE IN HIS JOY

He will spread his wings over you and keep
you secure. His faithfulness is like
a shield or a city wall.

PSALM 91:4 CEV

Father, my spirit and mind are at rest when
I fully realize that You have my life covered.
I'm not in control, I see that full well, and I
take joy in knowing that Your faithful love
is my protection and peace. Because You
are near, I can delight in this day and walk
freely in the safety and care that You give.
In Your name I pray, Jesus.

AMEN.

JOY FOR THE DOWNCAST

Let the bones you have crushed rejoice.

PSALM 51:8

Father, I pray for people I know who don't
have joy—whose spirits are crushed from
the weight of this world. Help me to be
a messenger of gladness in You to erase
the sadness that wants to overtake them.
Help me to show them there is hope and
more to live for than the shallow and false
promises that constantly disappoint. Give
me courage to be a light of Your joy to
spread seeds of love that bring healing and
comfort that is real and true.
All praise to You.

AMEN.

JULY

FREEDOM

LIVING FREE

Now the Lord is the Spirit, and where the
Spirit of the Lord is, there is freedom.

II CORINTHIANS 3:17

Lord, when I read this verse I can't help but
feel excited, because Your Spirit lives in me!
That means there are no excuses: I am truly
free. Free from the guilt of my past sinful
ways, free from the oppression of fear, free
from worry and doubt. I am free to receive
Your love with all my heart. I am free to
walk in strength and confidence that You
are with me always. Free to live with joy—
Your joy—all because You live in me.
Thanks be to God.

AMEN.

FORWARD FREEDOM

For freedom, Christ set us free.
Stand firm then and don't submit again
to a yoke of slavery.
GALATIANS 5:1

Lord, I love that You not only set me free
from the sins of my past, You command
me to stand firm and strong in my freedom
today. So the next time I am tempted to
return to a guilty state or succumb to
shameful thoughts, help me to remember
I've been forgiven, and there's no turning
back. Help me not to look back—to only live
forward in the power and victory
that You provide.

AMEN.

FREEDOM TO CHOOSE

"Everything is permissible," but not
everything is beneficial. "Everything is
permissible," but not everything builds up.

I CORINTHIANS 10:23

Father, these are such wise words—help me
to keep them fresh in my thoughts. There is
freedom in having choices, but sometimes
there are so many I get confused and
distracted from what is pleasing to You.
Help me to choose carefully what is
beneficial to both myself and to others so I
can relax and enjoy whatever I'm doing with
a clear conscience and peace of mind. In
Your great name.

AMEN.

FREE TO WORSHIP

They will hand you over to local courts,
and you will be flogged in the synagogues.
You will stand before governors and kings
because of Me.

MARK 13:9

Father, I am grateful to live in a country
where I am free to worship You without
persecution or trouble. I know this is not
the case in many other countries, so I don't
take it for granted. I pray for Christians
around the world who are imprisoned and
beaten for believing in You. Give them hope
and courage to keep on, and give me the
mind to keep them covered in prayer.
In Jesus' name.

AMEN.

FREEDOM IN TRUTH

Then Jesus said to the Jews who had
believed Him, "If you continue in My word,
you really are My disciples."

JOHN 8:31

Father, I have come to know that it is not
only important to read Your Word but vital
to do what it says. That means putting Your
purposes before my own, but, I confess,
that is not always easy. Help me get my
"self" out of the way and remember that
Your Word is truth, and that truth sets me
free from all the lies and distractions I am
faced with by this world. Your ways are so
much better than mine. I want the world to
see a difference, to see a reflection of Your
light in my life.

AMEN.

NO LONGER SLAVES

I am the Lord your God who brought you out of the land of Egypt, so that you would be slaves no longer; I have broken your chains so that you can walk with dignity.

LEVITICUS 26:13 TLB

Father, it blesses my heart to know that You want me to walk and live with dignity. And the only way I can do that is if I am free from all oppression. In You, my enemies can no longer touch me; temptations no longer have the power they once had. I'm able to live with my chin held high because You have destined me to. Thank You for breaking all chains of fear, doubt, worry, and shame. You are God, and I love that I am Yours.

AMEN.

FREE OF FEAR

For God has not given us a spirit of fear, but
one of power, love, and sound judgment.

II TIMOTHY 1:7

Lord, many days, many moments I hold
back from really living because of fear.
Sometimes I don't even realize I'm afraid
until I find myself watching others pursue
their dreams while I stay comfortable on
the sidelines. I no longer want to hold back,
because fear is not of You—and it keeps
me from experiencing true joy and peace.
I call upon You now to lift me out of my
fear and free me to run toward fulfilling the
complete and true purpose You created me
for. In Jesus' name.

AMEN.

FREEDOM MEANS CONFIDENCE

For you were called to freedom, brothers
and sisters; only do not use your freedom
as an opportunity to indulge your flesh.
GALATIANS 5:13 NET

Father, Your grace is the greatest gift I've
ever experienced. It has set me free from
the condemnation I used to carry in my
heart. I am filled with new confidence
knowing that when I make a mistake, You
won't hold it over me like a weight to drag
me down. Help me remember, though, that
Your grace is not an excuse to do whatever
I want. It is a gift to draw from out of
sincere desire to remain in Your great
and holy presence.
AMEN.

FREEDOM FROM WHAT OTHERS THINK

God paid a great price for you.
So don't become slaves of anyone else.
I CORINTHIANS 7:23 CEV

Lord, it's hard to conceive the thought of being someone's slave in this day and time, but to be a people pleaser, a peace keeper, is a form of slavery. To worry about what others think of me, to fret over whether or not someone likes me is indeed not living free. Yes, I should be at peace with others to the best of my ability, but You, and only You, are the One I want to live for and from whom I want to hear, "Well done; with you I am very pleased." In Jesus' name.

AMEN.

FREE TO LIVE BOLDLY

They promise them freedom,
but they themselves are slaves of
corruption, since people are enslaved
to whatever defeats them.

II PETER 2:19

Lord, there are so many things to defeat
my purpose in life, especially when people
who don't know You skillfully entice me to
want to live the way they do. Please guard
my heart and mind from false promises and
help me to live in this world without being
of it. It's only in You that my spirit is light
and free to live bold and unashamed to
proclaim that You are the way,
the truth, and the life.

AMEN.

FREEDOM IN HIS GRACE

Since God's grace has set us free from the
law, does that mean we can go on sinning?
Of course not!

ROMANS 6:15 NLT

Father, I'm so thankful I can go through
each day without worrying that a giant
gavel is going to slam down whenever I
think or do something I know I shouldn't.
Your love, Your grace is overflowing—it is
generous and constant, and it washes over
me now. Help me to walk in the freedom
of Your grace today and remember the
sacrifice that was made on my behalf
so that I could experience it. Your
lovingkindness is a treasure to me.
Thank You, Jesus.

AMEN.

FREEDOM IN JESUS

He has sent me to heal the brokenhearted,
to proclaim liberty to the captives
and freedom to the prisoners.

ISAIAH 61:1

Lord, when I think of prison, I think of
more than a jail cell where people live
because they've broken the law. I think of
the bondage of fear, the pit of despair, the
shackles of shame, and the tethers that
hold back my hope of victory over the lies
I've believed about myself and about You.
But You sent Jesus! He overcame them
all! He's brought healing for my heart and
dignity for my life. Since knowing Your
Son and receiving Him as my own Savior,
I am free to live as You intended all along.
Thanks be to You.

AMEN.

GUILT FREE

[Jesus] stood up and said to them,
"The one without sin among you should be
the first to throw a stone at her."

JOHN 8:7

Jesus, thank You that, by Your grace and
forgiveness, I am no longer condemned.
I can live guilt free from the eternal
consequences of my sin. Help me to
remember this the next time my thoughts
say otherwise, the next time someone
speaks to me as though I am less than the
princess You say I am. Help me to throw
off the lies and the weight that comes with
untruths and instead live free in Your truth
and Your love. In Your wonderful name.

AMEN.

FREEDOM IN RIGHTEOUSNESS

Thank God that, although you used to be
slaves of sin, you obeyed from the heart
that pattern of teaching to which you were
handed over, and having been set free from
sin, you became enslaved to righteousness.

ROMANS 6:17-18

Father, it seems so contradictory to want
to be enslaved to anything, yet to be held
captive by You and Your saving grace is
nothing less than sublime. Your ways are
righteous; Your ways are truth; Your ways
are perfect; so without You, my purpose
and being are lost to an imperfect world. I
cling to You this day, trusting and believing
and walking in the freedom I have under
Your generous and loving care.

AMEN.

FREEDOM TO PRAY

Then King David went in,
sat in the LORD's presence, and said...

II SAMUEL 7:18

Lord, who am I that I get to enter into
Your presence—the very One who created
the universe and everything in it? I, of all
people...I can approach Your throne and
spill out my heart to Your listening ear and
compassionate heart. Thank You for the
freedom to pray, the freedom to run to You
with my cares and struggles, my worship
and praise. You are not a distant, far-off
God—You are here and near to me now.
Thank You for the gift of Your presence.
All glory to You.

AMEN.

FREEDOM IN HEALING

For you that honor my name, victory will
shine like the sun with healing in its rays,
and you will jump around like calves at play.
MALACHI 4:2 CEV

Lord, I am so grateful for healing and
the freedom it brings. I'm not just talking
about healing for physical ailments but for
emotional and spiritual injuries—the results
of unseen battles over the months and
years that still try to tear me apart inside.
I bring my wounds and scars to You—for
cleansing, repair, restoration, and renewal.
Lift my burdens of pain and release me
to new heights of life and ministry I could
never attain on my own.
To You be the glory.
AMEN.

FREE TO DREAM

Faith is the reality of what is hoped for,
the proof of what is not seen.

HEBREWS 11:1

Father, to believe in and aim toward
the dreams You've placed in my heart
is exhilarating. The thought of actually
working to fulfill them can be scary. I know
I need more faith to trust You more—to
remove the obstacles of doubt and fear
and instill in me greater hope for each day.
I want to take the next step of faith and
experience the power of Your presence in
accomplishing what others deem to be the
impossible. You don't just give dreams,
You fulfill them as well.
All praise and glory to You.

AMEN.

FREEDOM IN BEING DEBT-FREE

Don't run up debts, except for the huge
debt of love you owe each other.
ROMANS 13:8 THE MESSAGE

Father, the burden of financial debt can be
so heavy and cause such anxiety as bills
begin to mount. Help me to live within my
means and learn to be content with what I
have. Help me to trust You more to help fill
my needs without having to borrow money
as a result. Help me to do what I can to
make ends meet, then trust You with what's
left. I know You love me and will provide
in Your own way and in Your perfect time.
Thank You for Your goodness and care.

AMEN.

FREEDOM IN FORGIVING

How joyful is the one whose transgression
is forgiven, whose sin is covered!

PSALM 32:1

Father, forgiving is very hard, but I know it's
necessary for having complete peace and
joy with You. Help me turn off the lies in my
head that keep telling me to hold a grudge
and to seek my own justice. You've forgiven
me for so many wrongdoings, I know that
forgiving others is the right thing to do.
But it's hard. Help me begin today first by
releasing my hurt to You. Soften my heart
as I place my offenders at the foot of Your
throne and trust You for healing, renewal,
and freedom from the anger I've been
carrying. In Jesus' name.

AMEN.

FREEDOM IN DEATH

For me, to live is Christ and to die is gain.
PHILIPPIANS 1:21

Lord, one of the greatest freedoms in life
is knowing that when I die to myself—my
agenda, my own selfish motives, my bad
habits—I am able to truly be and do and
live in a way that brings amazing joy and
satisfaction. That's because when I get
myself out of the way, You are at the center
of my everything, and I am able to fully rest
in Your trusting hands. Lead me, guide me,
and show me Your plans because I know
they are far better than anything I could
imagine. To live means You are at the center
of me. In Jesus' name.

AMEN.

FREEDOM IN TRUTH

You will know the truth,
and the truth will set you free.
JOHN 8:32 CEV

Father, I love Your Word because it's
filled with truth—truth for knowing Your
heart, knowing how to live, and knowing
safeguards to take for being safe within
Your care. When my mind is free from lies
from the enemy—the kind that cause doubt
and worry, fear and shame—I am free to
simply be and rest my soul in spite of being
in a very chaotic world. Thank You for Your
truth and the saving grace it is for my heart.
All glory to You.

AMEN.

FREEDOM TO ASK

A heart that has peace is life to the body,
but wrong desires are like the wasting away
of the bones.

PROVERBS 14:30 NLV

Lord, I know that when I lack peace, it's
because I've either done something I know I
shouldn't have, or my focus is on something
other than You. I want to turn my thoughts
and fix them on You now. Please help me
to keep You at the forefront and to walk
straight to You. I want, I need, Your peace
today—I need it to feel truly free from all
the what-ifs that vie for my attention.
I praise You and ask for peace
in Jesus' name.
AMEN.

FREEDOM IN
THE RIGHT FEAR

The fear of the LORD is a fountain of life.

PROVERBS 14:27

Father, I'm so glad You aren't a God of
punishment, but one of redemption and
grace. I'm so glad You aren't a God who
imprisons, but one who sets captives free
through forgiveness. I'm so glad I have
nothing to fear in You, but can approach
Your throne and receive life and love for
always. I'm so glad You are my God. I revere
and worship all that You are—and You are
wonderful. In Jesus' great name.

AMEN.

FREEDOM IN CONTENTMENT

In any and every circumstance I have
learned the secret of contentment.

PHILIPPIANS 4:12 NET

Lord, I confess I constantly struggle with
being content and wanting for nothing. My
problem is, I compare my life with someone
else's and then feel dissatisfied. I'm so sorry.
You have blessed me beyond measure, and
I am truly grateful. Help me to keep my
mind on what I have to be thankful for and
the abundance You have shown toward me.
I love You and, even better, I know You love
me. Thank You from my heart.

AMEN.

FREE FROM CARES

Humble yourselves...casting all your cares
on Him, because He cares about you.

I PETER 5:6-7

Father, I cast my cares on You right now.
They are too heavy for me to hold—I'm not
capable of solving any of them on my own.
Please take them one by one and release
me from the burden they've been. I want to
walk free in Your love this very moment and
throughout the day. Cleanse me from doubt
and worry and fill me with Your presence
and hope. Help me to resist any temptation
to take them back—I have cast them to You
once and for all. In Jesus I pray.

AMEN.

FREE TO START FRESH EVERY DAY

He redeems me from death...He fills my life with good things. My youth is renewed like the eagle's!

PSALM 103:4-5 NLT

Lord, when I really claim and live in the promise of Your forgiveness, there is a surge of relief and new strength like no other. You've removed guilt from my conscience; You've restored my broken spirit; You've redeemed time lost to wayward living; and You've proven to me time and again how much You love me. How can I not want to soar into the fresh wind of life You give me every day?! Thank You from the core of my heart.

AMEN.

FREEDOM IN RIGHT LIVING

Point out anything You find in me that makes You sad, and lead me along the path of everlasting life.

PSALM 139:24 TLB

Father, I want to please You. I want You to smile into my life and make me holy. Because when You do, I am free from the enemy's hold on my life and able to experience true intimacy with You. Please show me anything I'm doing or thinking that offends You, and help me to stop doing it. I want to walk in the full hope and joy of living free within Your ways and truths. To You be all praise.

AMEN.

FREEDOM FROM THE PAST

Brothers and sisters...I do this one thing:
I forget about the things behind me and
reach out for the things ahead of me.

PHILIPPIANS 3:13 CEB

Father, when I think about my past and the
way I lived—the rebellion, the pride, and the
disregard for You—I shudder and fight not
to feel embarrassed and ashamed. But You
have freed me from my guilt. Your grace
covers me and Your sacrifice protects me
from the condemnation I would otherwise
have faced. Help me not to look back but
stay focused on what is ahead—a future full
of great possibilities filled with Your love
and favor. All praise to You.

AMEN.

FREE FROM CONDEMNATION

When you are directed by the Spirit,
you are not under obligation
to the law of Moses.
GALATIANS 5:18 NLT

Jesus, sometimes it's hard to comprehend
that when I accepted You as my Savior,
Your Spirit came into me and took up
residence! I am fully alive with Your very
breath and so thankful for Your forgiveness
and grace that now cover me. I no longer
face condemnation—I've been released
from my sinful past and now live in freedom
for eternity. Thank You for the sacrifice You
made on my behalf and for the gift of new
life in You. All glory and honor to You.
AMEN.

UNITED AND FREE

David marched out with the army
and was successful in everything
Saul sent him to do.

I SAMUEL 18:5

Lord, thank You for the freedom I have
living in the United States of America. So
many have sacrificed their very lives so that
I can worship You, have independence of
mind, and go wherever I want whenever I
feel like it. Please keep our states united
and strong for generations to come. Help
me to be a promoter of peace and a
disciple of truth—Your truth—to keep the
torchlight of our service men and women
burning bright into the future.
All glory to You.

AMEN.

FREEDOM FOR ALL OF ETERNITY

But The lovingkindness of the LORD is from
everlasting to everlasting on those who
[reverently] fear Him.

PSALM 103:17 AMP

Father, I praise You with all my heart for
knowing I am Yours and that I will be with
You through all of eternity. This helps me to
keep my perspective more on the eternal
and less on my day-to-day struggles. Thank
You for saving me, for setting me free from
my old self and the ways of this world.
You are life and love that I carry
in my heart with great thanksgiving.
Praise and love to You.

AMEN.

AUGUST

REST

REST FROM DEMANDS

[Jesus] said to them,
"Come away by yourselves to a remote
place and rest for a while." For many people
were coming and going, and [the disciples]
did not even have time to eat.

MARK 6:31

O Lord, I know You understand the pressure
I feel with all the demands that are placed
on me each day. The list seems endless and
my strength and willpower are strained.
Please show me the unnecessary burdens
I'm putting on myself, and give me
Your strength to complete the tasks that
are truly important for today.
In Your Spirit I pray.

AMEN.

REST IN TRUST

Trust in the LORD with all your heart,
and do not rely on your own understanding;
in all your ways know Him,
and He will make your paths straight.
PROVERBS 3:5-6

Lord, I take in a deep breath now and
exhale all of me that I can. I want to be
filled by more of You and less of me. Help
me to rest in the knowledge that You are
with me and involved in every detail of my
life story. I can trust You with every fiber of
my being. Help me to let go of me and my
agenda and trust in Your love and
perfect way for this day.
In Your sweet name.
AMEN.

REST FROM THE CHAOS

God is not a God of disorder but of peace.
I CORINTHIANS 14:33

O God, life today is so chaotic. It's
hard to watch the news without feeling
overwhelmed, and it's hard to live without
feeling as though I'm always behind. Please
come into this day with Your peace and
calm. Bring order to my thoughts and
control to my emotions. Surround me with
the serenity of Your presence. Let it be
bigger and stronger than all the distractions
that vie for my energy. Help me rest by
staying in perfect stride with Your Spirit on
the path You have set before me.
Oh, how I love You.
AMEN.

REST IN HIS LOVE

Because the king trusts in the Lord,
he will never stumble, never fall;
for he depends upon the steadfast love of
the God who is above all gods.

PSALM 21:7 TLB

Father, I can't imagine living without Your
constant love. It's true, it's pure, it's healing,
and it's always here for me, no matter what.
Your love holds me up when I can't take
another step on my own. It surrounds and
protects me from temptation and harm.
I need it for my very life. I want to rest in
Your steadfast love today as if it's the most
important thing in my world, because it is.
In Your holiness I pray.

AMEN.

REST FROM WORRIES

Don't worry about your life,
what you will eat or what you will drink....
But seek first the kingdom of God and
His righteousness, and all these things will
be provided for you.

MATTHEW 6:25, 33

Lord, I know that when I worry, it's because
my focus is on my troubles and not on
Your greatness. Help me to seek Your face
today and rest in complete faith that You
are already filling my needs and working
to solve my problems. I want simply to
take You at Your word when You say not to
worry and to believe with all my heart that
You will provide at just the right time. In
Your great name.

AMEN.

REST IN HIS CARE

Humble yourselves, therefore, under the
mighty hand of God, so that He may exalt
you at the proper time, casting all your
cares on Him, because He cares about you.

I PETER 5:6-7

Father, I'm so glad You aren't a far-off God,
but are intimate and close and aware of
all that weighs on my heart. I want to curl
up in Your mighty right hand and close my
eyes in complete trust in Your care. Help
me carry this thought throughout my day
and remember that You are in control and
that You have the very best in store for me
ahead. I trust in You.

AMEN.

REST ON THE SABBATH

The Lord blessed the Sabbath day
and declared it holy.

EXODUS 20:11

Father, it's so easy to keep busy every day
of the week—it's no wonder I am so often
tired. Help me to guard one day, Your day,
for resting my body and mind, and for
worshiping You for all Your goodness and
glory. I know I am better for it, and You are
pleased when I do. Thank You for rest, true
and holy rest. All praise be to You.

AMEN.

REST FROM
FAST-PACED LIVING

Our God says, "Calm down,
and learn that I am God!"

PSALM 46:10 CEV

Lord, life is always so fast. Every day flies,
and I'm often unsure what all the activity
is even for. And, I'm so sorry to say, I miss
You in so much of each day because I
constantly hurry from one thing to the next.
Please help me slow down. Help me
prioritize what's truly important and let the
rest go. I want to breathe deeper and enjoy
my time walking and working completely in
sync with You, sharing each moment with
You. In Your love I pray.

AMEN.

REST IN HONEST WORK

Seek to lead a quiet life, to mind your own
business, and to work with your own hands,
as we commanded you, so that you may...
not be dependent on anyone.

I THESSALONIANS 4:11-12

Father, sometimes the dailiness of work
feels monotonous, and I wonder if I am
really making a difference to anyone. Help
me to remember that all I do is for You—
that I'm to work as though I am working
for You. When I do, I feel tremendous
satisfaction knowing I have done my best,
that I'm right where You want me to be, and
that the results are in Your hands to do with
what You will. I lift my praise to You.

AMEN.

REST FROM TECHNOLOGY

They feared the LORD but also served their
idols. Still today, their children
and grandchildren continue doing
as their fathers did.

II KINGS 17:41

Father, I spend so much time on my
computer and phone, I'm afraid at times
they have more control over me than I
have over them. And sometimes I feel more
connected with the world than I do with
You. Help me to have better balance—help
me turn off my devices and spend time
praying and reading Your Word and simply
enjoying Your presence more. Help me to
keep in perspective that they are tools and
nothing more. You are the One true Source
of my fulfillment and lasting joy.
All praise be to You.

AMEN.

REST IN GRACE

My grace is sufficient for you,
for My power is perfected in weakness.

II CORINTHIANS 12:9

O Father, thank You for the gift of Your
grace. Forgive me for forgetting that I
am to walk in it every day. Help me to
remember that it's okay to be weak,
because when I am, I'm more reliant on You
than ever. Help me to stop beating myself
up for mistakes I've made and instead hold
on to the full measure of grace You have
instilled in my life. I want to rest in knowing
that I am not alone. You are with me and
You have me covered.
In Your great name I pray.

AMEN.

REST FROM INJUSTICE

He is a shield for those who live
with integrity so that he may guard
the paths of justice.

PROVERBS 2:7-8

Father, all around I see so many injustices.
Life here on earth truly isn't fair for all.
Seeing wicked people prosper, innocent
lives suffer, and the proud be praised—I
confess it's taxing on my soul. I remember,
though, that You are a just God. And You
promise to balance the scales of injustice in
Your time and in Your way. Help me to rest
from my inner drive to take matters into my
own hands, but instead focus on Your lead
and trust that You're in control.

AMEN.

REST IN HIS GOODNESS

His divine power has given us everything
required for life and godliness through the
knowledge of Him who called us by His own
glory and goodness.

II PETER 1:3

Father, You are so very good—You provide
so abundantly for all that I need. Whether
it's wisdom, understanding, strength, food,
rest, grace, forgiveness, or love, You give
all so freely to overflowing. I cannot thank
You enough for blessing me the way You
do. Forgive me for any ounce of worry I still
hold on to in spite of all of Your kindness.
Today I will rest in Your care and dwell on
Your goodness to me.

AMEN.

REST IN KNOWING

I am the LORD. I have called you
for a righteous purpose,
and I will hold you by your hand.

ISAIAH 42:6

Father, I think on all the promises You've
written in Your Word, and I believe that You
will keep them. I have believed for some
time, but now I want to step from believing
You will into a place of knowing You have.
You've already planned the answers to the
mountains I face. You even hear my cries
before I hear them myself. The peace that
washes over my soul for knowing this is
indescribable. Help me to rest in that peace
today. All glory and praise to You.

AMEN.

REST IN CREATION

I will meditate about your glory, splendor,
majesty, and miracles.

PSALM 145:5 TLB

Lord, I love the beauty of Your creation
and the oneness with You I feel when I'm
in it. The sound of water flowing, the smell
of pine and cedar, the quiet waves of wind
flowing through trees, the birds bursting
forth in song...Meditating on it releases me
to breathe deeper and exhale all the stress
from my body. Thank You for the blessing
of nature—it reveals a lovely and pleasing
part of Your nature for all to enjoy. In the
beauty of Your presence I pray.

AMEN.

REST FROM THE NOISE

He withdrew from there in a boat to a
secluded place by Himself.
MATTHEW 14:13 NASB

Jesus, there were times You withdrew
from the crowds and the noise to be alone
with the Father, and I want the same for
myself. There is noise all around, from TV,
radio, construction, vehicles—the clamor
is everywhere, and I need to unplug and
just be quiet. Remind me to make time to
withdraw, to disconnect, and to immerse
myself in the peaceful rest that You give. I
only want to hear Your voice and feel the
soothing balm it is for my spirit. I humbly
ask this in Your name.
AMEN.

REST IN QUIET

He lets me lie down in green pastures;
He leads me beside quiet waters.

PSALM 23:2

Father, will You lead me to quiet waters
today? Even in the midst of my demanding
pace of life and clamoring noise all round,
will You lead me to the quietness of Your
heart? I want to feel every beat and hear
each whisper You put into my mind. Slow
my steps and guide my way so I'm in
perfect step with Your will. Help me rest in
Your presence and perfect peace.
In You I am whole and renewed.

AMEN.

REST FROM SORROW

My soul is weary with sorrow;
strengthen me according to Your word.
PSALM 119:28 NIV

Father, I need Your joy in a world that
is hard and heavy. So much devastation
surrounds me, and I don't see signs of
things getting any better. Please give
me Your strength and power to resist
the temptation to get discouraged and
depressed. Fill me with courage and
hope that I can share with others who
are struggling in life. Help me to rest
and remember that You are carrying me,
so I don't have to carry life's burdens
on my own. Thank You for Your loving,
outstretched arm toward me this day.
AMEN.

REST IN FORGIVENESS

There is forgiveness of sins
for all who repent.
LUKE 24:47 NLT

Father, I'm so very grateful for the
forgiveness I have as Your child. To know
that sin won't be held against me is a
glorious relief. The weight of guilt that's
lifted, the joy I'm able to have, the closeness
I'm able to experience with You—all
because I'm forgiven. Please examine my
heart now and see if there is any offensive
way in me. Convict me of change I need
to make for my benefit and others', and
bless me with the continual cleansing Jesus
brings. In Your sweet name I pray.
AMEN.

REST FROM STRIVING

What do people get for all the toil
and anxious striving with which
they labor under the sun?
ECCLESIASTES 2:22 NIV

Lord, I truly need Your help to stop striving.
I know that when I do—and that is often—
it's because I want something in my own
timing and in my own way. I bring urgency
to situations that aren't urgent, and I try to
force events and people out of the natural
state that You've preordained. I trust in
You. I want Your way and lead for this day.
Therefore I will wait and act when You say
it's time. In the meantime, I am thankful to
rest from striving. With thanksgiving I pray.
AMEN.

REST IN HIS REDEMPTION

Into your hand I entrust my spirit;
you have redeemed me, LORD, God of truth.

PSALM 31:5

Father, thank You for redeeming me and
all the mistakes and wandering of my past.
You have breathed new life into what was
once dead; You have worked Your good
into the wrongs I've done; You've brought
healing to places of my heart that were
broken; and You've removed the guilt and
shame I used to carry. You've restored what
I thought was ruined. I put my hope and
trust in You now and for eternity.
Only You are worthy.

AMEN.

REST FROM THE NEED TO PERFORM

Even when we were God's enemies,
He made peace with us,
because His Son died for us.

ROMANS 5:10 CEV

Lord, I read Your Word and know that You love me just the way I am, yet I struggle with feeling as though I've got to do more, be more, and accomplish more in order to even love myself, let alone receive Your love. Help me to truly grasp that Your love is not conditional—You want me and love me as I am. Help me turn off the lies in my mind that say otherwise, and help me to embrace the me You made, just as I am.

AMEN.

REST IN HOPE

Rest in God alone, my soul,
for my hope comes from Him.

PSALM 62:5

Father, there are so many things that vie
for what and where I place my hope. And I
confess that some are very appealing and
tempting. But I've learned that there is
only One true source from which real hope
comes, and that is You. So I rest in You
today—not another person or a full bank
account or calm circumstances but in You,
no matter what. My eyes are on You.
In Jesus' name.

AMEN.

REST IN HIS VICTORY

All the ends of the earth
have seen our God's victory.

PSALM 98:3

Father, thank You for the rest that is mine
because Jesus has overcome the world.
He has brought victory for all of humanity.
And now I can rest in knowing I am mighty
through His Spirit; I have escaped death
because of His scars. There may be battles
on this earth while I am here, but the final
war has already been won.

All praise be to Jesus.

AMEN.

REST IN GOD'S WORD

O Lord, your instructions endure;
they stand secure in heaven.
PSALM 119:89 NET

Father, I know I can always rest in whatever
Your Word says to me, because it's the one
Source of truth that exists. Whenever I read
it, You breathe life into my very spirit and
open my eyes to Your faithfulness and love.
It will stand forever in time because You are
eternal; it will never change because You
remain the same. It's a precious gift to have
access to Your heart and to learn as much
about You as I desire. With thanksgiving
in my heart.
AMEN.

REST FROM A BROKEN HEART

The LORD is near the brokenhearted;
he saves those crushed in spirit.

PSALM 34:18

Lord, so many things today break my
heart—from relationships that have
ended, to the passing of loved ones, to
the anguish-inducing news headlines. But
instead of grieving another day, I want to
rejoice—in Your goodness and mercy, in
Your grace and love. I'm so grateful for the
renewal and hope You give. Will You help
me focus on all that is good and life giving
today? Help me see the sweet and simple
blessings You offer, and to rest in knowing I
am not alone. Thank You, Jesus.

AMEN.

REST IN A SURRENDERED LIFE

For me, to live is Christ and to die is gain.

PHILIPPIANS 1:21

Lord, I give my heart to You. Please take it
and mend its broken and bruised pieces.
Please smooth the jagged edges. I want my
life to be in Your hands. I surrender to Your
call. You are love, and I am in great need.
You are life, and I can't do mine on my own.
So please take me and grow me, mold me
and use me—my life isn't life without Your
breath beating in my heart. I am Yours, and
I rest within the peace I have in You.

AMEN.

REST FROM ADVERSITY

So David left Gath and took refuge
in the cave of Adullam.

I SAMUEL 22:1

Father, sometimes my problems feel so big,
I feel overtaken and overwhelmed. I need
Your help; I want to escape into Your arms.
Please carry me today and guard me from
the ocean wave that keeps wanting to beat
down on me. Keep me safe in the shadow
of Your wings, and guard me from the
enemy's attempts to discourage me. I want
to rest my weary soul in You. Thank You for
Your great love.

AMEN.

REST IN GOD'S PROMISES

Through these He gave us the very great
and precious promises. With these gifts you
can share in God's nature, and the world
will not ruin you with its evil desires.

II PETER 1:4 NCV

Lord, there are lies being told everywhere I
go. And it is so hard to know who or what
to trust and believe. This is why I continually
turn to Your Word—to filter the lies and
keep Your promises of love, wisdom,
provision, and grace at the forefront of
my mind. I sigh out the confusion and
breathe in Your faithful words that keep
me grounded and protected from believing
untruths. By the power I have
in Jesus' name I pray.

AMEN.

REST IN RECONCILIATION

At that moment the curtain of the temple
was torn in two from top to bottom.

MATTHEW 27:51 NIV

Father, I'm so grateful to You for sending
Jesus to this world. Because of His sacrifice
and resurrection, I am reconciled to You,
the Creator of the universe and lover of my
soul. There is no longer a veil separating
You from humanity. We are together, and
nothing can separate us from Your love. I
am able to pray to You any time of day or
night. I have the hope of spending eternity
with You and Your Spirit to help me until
that day. Thank You for blessing my soul
with the knowledge that I am reconciled
with You. All glory and praise to You.

AMEN.

REST IN JESUS

Take up My yoke and learn from Me,
because I am lowly and humble in heart,
and you will find rest for your souls.

MATTHEW 11:29

Jesus, I want You and need You today. You
are the only One to bring pure and holy
peace into my difficult and often confusing
life. My gaze is on You—I will follow where
You lead. I take Your words to heart
because You are the best Friend I've ever
known. I love Your ways and want to live
them out for myself. I trust You with my life
because You are my very life. You are all
that is good, and I rest in You.
In Your great name I pray.

AMEN.

SEPTEMBER

VICTORY

VICTORY IN CHRIST

If you confess with your mouth, "Jesus is Lord," and believe in your heart that God raised him from the dead, you will be saved.

ROMANS 10:9

Jesus, I believe—I believe that You are Lord and that You sacrificed Your life on behalf of mine. It is very humbling and blessed to meditate on this truth. I am so extremely grateful. I lift up my life, my heart, my thoughts, and my worship to You, my wonderful and loving Savior. Because of You and the power of Your Holy Spirit within me, I can live victoriously on this earth with the lasting hope of spending eternity with You. All glorious praise and honor to You.

AMEN.

VICTORY OVER WORRY

Do not worry about anything,
but pray and ask God for everything
you need, always giving thanks.

PHILIPPIANS 4:6 NCV

Father, forgive me for worrying about
anything. I know that when I do, it's a sign
that I am not fully trusting in You and that
I'm trying to figure out my circumstances
using my own logic. You have blessed me
so abundantly, I know that You love me and
are with me now working out things for my
good and Your glory. I thank You for Your
goodness and ask in faith for Your help with
the challenges I'm facing right now.
I trust in You, dear Jesus.

AMEN.

VICTORY IN CONTENTMENT

About midnight Paul and Silas were praying and singing hymns to God, and the prisoners were listening to them.

ACTS 16:25

Lord, if Paul and Silas could be content and sing in a prison cell, I believe I can sing and praise You in spite of the circumstances and challenges I face. Help me not to compare my life with others'; help me to dwell on my many blessings and choose to walk in Your joy. Help me remember that You are very much in control and to watch for Your loving touches throughout my day. In You, and only You, I will be content.

AMEN.

VICTORY OVER FEAR

God did not give us a Spirit of fear but of
power and love and self-control.
II TIMOTHY 1:7 NET

Lord, when I really think about it, fear
is such a part of my life. Decisions are
motivated by it, and so much of life is lost
because of it. Help me to remember that
fear is not of You and that I actually have
Your Spirit of power to help me overcome.
Help me to draw from Your power now.
I have nothing to fear, believing and
knowing I'm in the palm of Your hand
and surrounded by Your presence.
I shall not be afraid. Thank You, Jesus,
for the gift of Your Spirit.
AMEN.

VICTORY IN KNOWING HIS LOVE

I am like an olive tree,
thriving in the house of God. I will
always trust in God's unfailing love.

PSALM 52:8 NLT

O God, basking in Your love sets me free
to truly live and grow and rejoice from my
heart. It's an indescribable love that fills
my heart with peace and burns like a flame
that spurs me to do and be as I've never
been before. It's a love that will never die or
wane. Your love will carry me into eternity
with You. Thank You for Your faithfulness.
My heart is so full.

AMEN.

VICTORY OVER SIN

Confess your sins to each other and pray
for each other so that you may be healed.
JAMES 5:16 CEB

Lord, it's hard to confess my sin—it makes
me feel vulnerable to possible judgment
and rejection. But You are loving, and
when I don't confess, I miss out on Your
supernatural healing and peace. So I
humbly bow my head and confess to You
now and ask for Your healing grace and
forgiveness. Help me also to extend the
same grace toward others so we can be
reconciled to You and to one another in
love. Together we can overcome and live
more fully in the power of prayer for each
other. In Jesus' precious name.
AMEN.

VICTORY IN HIS FORGIVENESS

He is so rich in kindness and grace that He purchased our freedom with the blood of His Son and forgave our sins.

EPHESIANS 1:7 NLT

Father, when I think of all the ways to sin—worry, envy, judging my neighbor, gossip, disobedience—I can see them all in myself to some degree. It's a wonder that You love me, or any of us, in our sin. But You do—so much so, You gave Your Son so that we can have forgiveness. Thank You for not leaving us to ourselves and the consequences we could be facing. Your lovingkindness provides a way to be close to You and to experience the fullness of Your love. Thank You for Jesus.

AMEN.

VICTORY IN EXTENDING FORGIVENESS

If you forgive those who sin against you,
your heavenly Father will forgive you.
MATTHEW 6:14 NLT

Father, it is hard to forgive others who've
hurt me—I'd much rather hold a grudge.
But Jesus clearly says I am to forgive. Help
me to fully grasp that forgiveness is for my
benefit as much as it is for others. Unless
I do, my wounds won't fully mend, and I
won't be able to walk in true freedom. I too
remember that You have forgiven me for
so many things, and I am called to a holy
standard of the same. I choose forgiveness,
Lord, and I walk in Your healing
grace today.
AMEN.

VICTORY OVER ADDICTION

I pray that He may grant you,
according to the riches of His glory,
to be strengthened with power
in your inner being through His Spirit.

EPHESIANS 3:16

Father, I pray this for myself—that You will
grant me strength through the power of
Your Spirit in me to overcome that which
controls me more than I control it. I am not
able on my own, but with You working and
moving within my mind and spirit, I can do
all things—one day at a time. Thank You for
the hope and the help that I need for today.
In the power of Jesus I pray.

AMEN.

VICTORY WHEN YOU CALL OUT TO GOD

When you call me and come
and pray to me, I will listen to you.
JEREMIAH 29:12 CEB

Father, I love that no matter what time
or place, when I call out to You, You hear.
You care. You are instantly listening with
Your full attention. This is a blessing to me
because there isn't anyone else I can share
every detail of what's on my mind and heart
and know it won't be shared and I won't be
judged. The calming peace You give assures
me that my prayers are received with
care and love, and I am blessed by Your
compassion and grace. I call out
to You now, Lord Jesus.
AMEN.

VICTORY IN TRUST

You will keep in perfect peace all who trust
in you, all whose thoughts are fixed on you!
ISAIAH 26:3 NLT

Lord, when I think on the ways You've
worked in my life and provided for my
needs, the trust I have in You is unshakable.
You have always come through. I may feel
anxious at times, but I know it's because
I'm thinking more about my problems than
Your faithfulness and love. Help me to
keep my thoughts on You today and rest
in knowing without a doubt that You are
working all things out for my good and
Your glory. In Jesus' name.
AMEN.

VICTORY OVER DARKNESS

I am the light of the world. Anyone who
follows Me will never walk in the darkness
but will have the light of life.

JOHN 8:12

Lord, there is darkness at every turn in this
world, and it's easy to get lost and lose
my way. The enemy is constantly trying
to throw me off course and make me lose
hope for my future. But Your Spirit in me
is alive—it shines to reveal Your presence
and gives direction for my path. Your
light reminds me that I am never alone
and that You are a power source that is
always burning and filling my heart with the
promise of hope for today, tomorrow,
and eternity. I am so very grateful.

AMEN.

VICTORY THROUGH FAITH

For truly I tell you, if you have faith
the size of a mustard seed...
Nothing will be impossible for you.

MATTHEW 17:20

Jesus, when I look at my life, I know I need
more faith. Not in my abilities or others', not
in a big paycheck or the stars, but in You.
Help me to step out now, believing You are
with me, that You are in control, and that
You won't let me fall. Help me move in the
direction I believe You are leading me, to do
what Your Spirit convicts me to do, and to
trust You with the outcome. I believe;
help my unbelief.

AMEN.

VICTORY FOR ENDURING THROUGH TRIALS

Don't try to squirm out of your problems.
For when your patience is finally in full
bloom, then you will be ready for anything,
strong in character, full and complete.

JAMES 1:4 TLB

Lord, that's exactly what I want to do—
squirm out of my problems! But I know
that in them, You are working in me a
greater hope, a stronger testimony, and
an unshakable faith. Forgive me for my
reluctance and complaining; create in
me a clearer eternal perspective that
overshadows my day-to-day hindrances.
Help me to shine Your love and light and
bring You glory through them all.
In Your name only.

AMEN.

VICTORY IN CHANGE

Let God change the way you think.
Then you will know how to do everything
that is good and pleasing to Him.

ROMANS 12:2 CEV

O God, how I struggle with controlling
my thoughts. They often control me by
running through constant "what ifs" and
"oh nos" to the point of exhaustion. Please
help me change the way I think. Give me
Your thoughts—the mind of Christ—which
is filled with power, strength, clarity, and
understanding. Fill each thought with
nuggets of truth from Your Word that are
calming, helpful, and hope-filled. I want to
stay—including my mind—in the center of
Your will for my life. Thank You
for Your great love.

AMEN.

VICTORY OVER JUDGMENT

Anyone who hears My Word and puts his trust in Him Who sent Me has life that lasts forever. He will not be guilty. He has already passed from death into life.

JOHN 5:24 NLV

Father, when I read this verse, my mind goes back to my life before I knew You. The guilt, the shame, the lack of hope...But You saved me! And now I have the hope of eternal life with You. My guilt is gone, and I am filled with life and love beyond what I ever knew to be possible. You are so very good, and I thank You from my heart for saving me. All praise and glory to You.

AMEN.

VICTORIOUS LIVING IN GRACE

We have all received grace upon grace
from His fullness, for the law was given
through Moses; grace and truth came
through Jesus Christ.

JOHN 1:16-17

Jesus, Your grace is one of the greatest
gifts I've ever been given. It's also one of
the hardest to grasp. It gives me all that I
need instead of all that I deserve. It heals
my heart with the fullness of Your love.
It catches and softens my stumbles and
doesn't keep track of wrongs. Lord, thank
You for Your indescribable grace. Help me
extend it to others with the same love and
passion You display in my life every day.
With thanksgiving in my heart.

AMEN.

VICTORY IN DAILY SERVICE

Each of you has been blessed with one of God's many wonderful gifts to be used in the service of others. So use your gift well.

I PETER 4:10 CEV

Father, give me a servant's heart. Open my eyes to who needs help and how I may serve through the power and leading of Your Spirit. Instill in me the same mercy and compassion You have for people, and give me the readiness to act, even in the smallest of ways, to love on others in their times of need. When I serve, I feel so full— of Your love, Your glory, and Your peace. So keep my willingness vigilant and my hands prepared to be an extension of You.

AMEN.

VICTORY IN A POOR SPIRIT

God blesses those people
who depend only on Him.
MATTHEW 5:3 CEV

Lord, I am at the end of myself and my
own resources—I need You. I've tried, and I
can't do life without You at the helm. I need
Your presence, Your love, Your peace, Your
healing—I need all of You in all of me. I give
You my junk and concerns and problems
and look to You to show me how to work
through them—in Your time and in Your
way. I just want You. Bless me with Your
peace. In Your name I pray.

AMEN.

VICTORY IN THE MIND OF CHRIST

We Christians actually do have
within us a portion of the very thoughts
and mind of Christ.

I CORINTHIANS 2:16 TLB

Jesus, my mind seems to be my biggest
enemy. It wanders, it focuses on negatives,
it tells me lies, and it's hard to make it
quiet. I call on Your Spirit within me now
to clear my mind of anything that isn't of
You. I want to hear Your voice. I want to
receive Your truth and wisdom for a godly
life. I want to hear Your whispers of love
spoken directly to my heart. Your thoughts
amaze me, and I want to hear them ring
throughout this day. In Your sweet name.

AMEN.

VICTORY FOR A CONTROLLED TONGUE

Those who guard their mouths and their
tongues guard themselves from trouble.
PROVERBS 21:23 CEB

Lord, my tongue has gotten me into trouble
I never saw coming. Sometimes I need a
muzzle—it's hard to tame it! Please put a
guard over it, put Your hand on it. Help me
to use better discretion with my words and
the way I speak them. Help me to edify
and encourage, say what You'd say, and
otherwise be still and be quiet. Help me
learn that sometimes the most powerful
thing I can say is nothing.
AMEN.

VICTORY IN PATIENCE

A person's insight gives him patience.
PROVERBS 19:11

Lord, You know I can be impatient. And I
know that when I am, it's because I want
something to happen in my way on my
timetable. But I know that You will not be
moved until You are ready. You have a much
bigger view of my life story, and I trust that
You are orchestrating circumstances now in
ways I cannot see, to my benefit. Help me
to draw from and rest in Your perspective.
Help me to have peace as I wait patiently
for Your hand to act and to move when the
time is perfect. In Your great name.

AMEN.

VICTORY IN BROKENNESS

If your heart is broken, you'll find GoD right
there; if you're kicked in the gut,
He'll help you catch your breath.
PSALM 34:18 THE MESSAGE

Father, painful points in life are inevitable
but so is Your presence. You've been with
me through every valley and crooked road.
And those have been times I've felt Your
Spirit seep into each crack and crevice of
my heart to hold it together and to keep it
beating. Your compassion is great;
Your mercy is unending. Your breath is life
giving and Your grace is sustaining.
Thank You for always being here for me.
In Your great love.
AMEN.

VICTORY IN GOD'S SILENCE

Trust in Him at all times, you people!
Pour out your hearts before Him!
PSALM 62:8 NET

Lord God, Your silence can be unbearable
at times. It challenges my trust in You at the
deepest level. But I do trust You. I know You
have Your reasons, and I do believe You are
working. Help me to be quiet as well and
to have patience and a listening ear. Grow
my faith to be constant and unwavering
and continually anticipating the sound of
Your voice once again. I know it will come,
because You are faithful.

AMEN.

VICTORY IN DRUDGERY

Whatever you do, do it from the heart,
as something done for the Lord
and not for people.

COLOSSIANS 3:23

Lord, I have come to learn that when I say
I want to serve You, that means I'm not to
place conditions on what that means. But
in the dailiness and monotonous routines,
the thankless tasks and quiet sacrifices, I
tend to forget whom I am really serving in
the end. It's Your words of "Well done" I
want to hear and the only ones that matter
on the deepest level. As long as You are
pleased, then I am too, no matter what
that means I'm to do. Thank You for the
privilege to serve.

AMEN.

VICTORY IN GIVING

"Bring the full tenth into the storehouse....
Test me in this way," says the Lord....
"See if I will not open the floodgates of
heaven and pour out a blessing for you
without measure."

MALACHI 3:10

Lord, when it comes to giving, my mind
tells me I won't have enough left to pay
my bills. Logic fights to thwart my faith in
Your provision. But giving doesn't have to
make sense, it just has to be, because when
I don't, I miss out on incredible blessings—
blessings that prove Your faithfulness, that
shine Your glory in my life, that reveal an
utter dependence on You that says I can't
but You can and will.

AMEN.

VICTORY IN OBEDIENCE

Adam caused many to be sinners
because he *disobeyed* God,
and Christ caused many to be made
acceptable to God because he *obeyed*.

ROMANS 5:19 TLB

Father, sometimes just hearing the word
obedience makes me cringe. You aren't a
God who stands over me with a scepter
shouting orders. You always give me a
choice to go my way or Yours. You gave
Adam a choice—and all of humanity has
suffered because of his disobedience.
Yet You sent Jesus—to His death—as the
ultimate example of obedience, and I am
saved because of it. So I choose to be
obedient to Your call, knowing You have my
supreme best at heart. In Christ's name.

AMEN.

VICTORY IN WAITING

Don't be impatient for the Lord to act!
Keep traveling steadily along His pathway
and in due season He will honor you
with every blessing.

PSALM 37:34 TLB

Lord, waiting can be so hard, but it does
get easier when I dwell on this promise
in Your Word. You are so good and Your
devotion rings true to my heart. So I will
wait—on Your perfect timing, Your perfect
way, Your perfect provision, and Your
perfect wisdom. And on the day I see You
act, I will rejoice in Your faithfulness and tell
everyone how You came through.
To You be all glory.

AMEN.

VICTORY IN KNOWING GOD'S WILL

As they were worshiping the Lord and
fasting, the Holy Spirit said...

ACTS 13:2

Father, I constantly seek Your will for my
life. Not just for my life as a whole, but also
in the day-to-day, because I know that what
I do today leads to tomorrow's results. But
sometimes it's hard to hear You, and I'm not
completely sure what You want me to do.
So I reach for Your heart. I yearn to be near
it, because I know that there I will discover
what's on it—for all of humanity and for me.
So show me Your heart, Lord. I want mine
to be as close to it as can be.

AMEN.

VICTORY IN JESUS

But thanks be to God, who gives us the
victory through our Lord Jesus Christ!

I CORINTHIANS 15:57

Jesus, thank You for the victory I have in
You in light of eternity! Your sacrifice has
not only changed my life, it's given me life.
You give me hope. You give me freedom.
You make a way where there is no way. Your
grace covers my broken life and transforms
me daily into a new creation. You are
wonderful and amazing, and I give You all
the glory for my blessed life.
In Your great name.

AMEN.

OCTOBER

PRAISE

PRAISE FOR A NEW DAY

This is the day the LORD has made;
let us rejoice and be glad in it.
PSALM 118:24

Father, please clear away all the distractions
and problems in my life and help me to
see only You. The sun is out; I have a roof
over my head; I am breathing; and I know
You love me. These, and so much more, are
reasons to simply be and rejoice in You this
day. I will be glad as I dwell in the peace
You give and the joy You provide for my
life. You have made another wonderful day,
and I am ready to live for You in it.
With a glad heart.
AMEN.

PRAISE FOR GOD'S GRACE

The Law stepped in to amplify the failure,
but where sin increased,
grace multiplied even more.
ROMANS 5:20 CEB

Jesus, because of You and the sacrifice You
made, I can live and walk in grace today
and every day. I don't deserve it, yet You
give it anyway straight from a heart of
compassion and mercy. Thank You for the
comfort in knowing my sins are forgiven
and I won't face eternal consequences—
You've faced them for me. I am humbled
and grateful and give You all praise for such
a selfless act of love. In Your precious name.
AMEN.

PRAISE FOR HIS PEACE

And the peace of God, which surpasses all
understanding, will guard your hearts
and minds in Christ Jesus.

PHILIPPIANS 4:7

Lord, I praise You that You are a God
of peace and that You share it with me
abundantly. It is a deep and abiding
state of tranquility in a chaotic and harsh
world. There is no explanation for it other
than Your very presence collides with my
cries for help and releases a supernatural
calmness that surrounds my heart and
keeps it safe. You give a "knowing" that all
will be okay. I worship You and
love You for Your peace.

AMEN.

PRAISE FOR HIS PROMISES

I am awake through each watch of the night
to meditate on Your promise.

PSALM 119:148

Father, I love Your Word—it is full of
promises I feel as though were written
just for me. You will never leave; You will
strengthen and help; Your mercies are new
every morning; there is nowhere I can go
to escape from Your love...I praise You from
the depths for such gifts for me to claim
and to meditate on every day and through
each night to assure me and give great
hope. My heart sings of love for You.

AMEN.

PRAISE FOR HIS CREATION

The heavens declare the glory of God,
and the expanse proclaims
the work of His hands.

PSALM 19:1

Lord, the heavens do declare Your glory,
and the earth proclaims every magnificent
stroke of Your hand in creation: the
splendor of the night sky, the glory in each
sunburst of dawn, the gorgeousness of the
forests and waterfalls, and the loveliness of
ocean beaches. Your presence is visible on
this earth, and Your Spirit moves my soul
with praise and delight. Thank You, Father,
for Your amazing creations.

AMEN.

PRAISE FOR HIS JOY

I [Jesus] have told you these things
so that My joy may be in you,
and your joy may be complete.

JOHN 15:11 NET

Jesus, thank You for the saving grace of
Your joy. To think that Your very joy—the joy
that You receive from the Father—is in me
now! It's almost unbelievable; it's hard to
grasp. What's wonderful is, no matter what
goes on around me, no matter the struggles
or difficulties, I am not left to myself to
wallow or live in fear. I am strengthened
with hope and led with joy in my heart to
keep moving and working out the calling
You have on my life. I am so grateful.

AMEN.

PRAISE FOR HIS FORGIVENESS

How blessed is the one whose rebellious
acts are forgiven, whose sin is pardoned!
PSALM 32:1 NET

Father, I am extremely blessed to know that
I am forgiven—for every selfish act, for not
loving my neighbor, for each careless word
spoken, for doing things my way instead of
Yours, and for the pride I have in thinking
I'm actually in control of my life. Instead
of living in fear of all the consequences, I
live in love knowing they've been removed
by Your Son. The weight of guilt, the
depression from shame no longer have
a place in my life. I praise You from the
depths for Your forgiveness.
AMEN.

PRAISE FOR HIS FAITHFULNESS

Because of the LORD's faithful love we do
not perish, for His mercies never end.
They are new every morning;
great is your faithfulness!

LAMENTATIONS 3:22-23

Father, You have been faithful since the
beginning of time—faithful in love and
faithful in redemption for a faithless and
wandering humanity. When I have rebelled,
You've not removed Your love. When I've
strayed, You've stayed right with me. When
I've started to fall, You've caught me in Your
mercy net and restored me to You. Your
righteous right hand has reached down
repeatedly to help and to heal my broken
life. I praise You from a very full heart.

AMEN.

PRAISE FOR HIS PROVISION

Now to Him who is able to do immeasurably
more than all we ask or imagine, according
to His power that is at work within us.

EPHESIANS 3:20 NIV

Lord, when I think on the amazing ways
You've provided, often far beyond what
I imagined, it's easy to praise You for not
only providing but for doing so with great
abundance. When Your floodgates of
goodness open, I'm continually amazed by
the wealth and richness You share, from
the intangible blessings—love, forgiveness,
purpose, hope—to the tangible ones—a
family, a place to live, a full pantry, and
work to do. I struggle to find words that
adequately express the depths of my
gratitude. All praise to You.

AMEN.

PRAISE FOR HIS HOLY SPIRIT

The...Holy Spirit, whom the Father will send
in My name, will teach you all things
and remind you of everything
I have told you.

JOHN 14:26

Jesus, little did everyone realize that when
You died on the cross, Your Spirit would
then become alive in all who believe in You.
I have Your power in me, and that is mind-
blowing. I praise You for such a gift. Forgive
me for the times I haven't let Your Spirit
be my driving force throughout each day. I
want to set Your presence within me aflame
right now and let You be the holy influence
to lead and guide my mind and actions.
To You be all glory.

AMEN.

PRAISE FOR HIS WORD

God's way is perfect. All the Lord's
promises prove true. He is a shield for all
who look to Him for protection.

PSALM 18:30 NLT

Father, I love Your Word. There is nothing
as trustworthy and true, exciting or
adventurous. Each book is a love letter
written straight from the depths of Your
heart. Your love, Your truths breathe life
into my very being and comfort into my
very soul. I turn to it for guidance and
wisdom and for learning You. The more I
know You, the more grounded I feel in Your
love and purpose for my life. It is a light to
my path in a dark and difficult world.
I praise You for Your Word.

AMEN.

PRAISE FOR HIS ARMOR

Put on all the armor that God gives,
so you can defend yourself against
the devil's tricks.
EPHESIANS 6:11 CEV

Lord, I'm so grateful that You don't leave
me to fight my daily battles ill-equipped.
You provide exactly the right armor for
what I need, depending on the fight I face.
Help me to remember to put it on—I often
forget! I never know how or when the
enemy will strike, and I know I need to be
on guard at all times. No matter how heated
or strong the fight gets, the power and
strength I have in You cannot be shaken.
All praise to You.
AMEN.

PRAISE FOR HIS HOLINESS

Holy, holy, holy is the Lᴏʀᴅ of Armies;
His glory fills the whole earth.

ISAIAH 6:3

Heavenly Father, holiness is the very
essence of Your being. And when Your
Holy Spirit washes over me, I cannot help
but worship You in the richness of Your
splendor and the fullness of Your joy. You
have no blemish or defect—You are perfect
and pure. I'm blessed to even enter Your
divine presence and am filled with praise to
call You Father. Please drop Your holy oil of
grace into the cistern of my heart to heal
and bless and remind me that I am Yours
for always. In Jesus' sweet name.

AMEN.

PRAISE FOR HIS HEALING

He heals the brokenhearted
and bandages their wounds.

PSALM 147:3

Jesus, I was so broken when I first came
to know You as Savior, and now, over time,
Your healing balm of mercy has changed
my heart. What used to be hard and
cracked is now soft and whole. You've not
only healed the battle scars of my mind,
You've transformed my entire being from
guilt and shame to one that is victorious
and free. Only You are worthy of all praise
for the restoration I've received through
forgiveness of sin and the covering of
Your grace. In You, Jesus, I pray.

AMEN.

PRAISE FOR HIS WISDOM

Now if any of you lacks wisdom, he should
ask God—who gives to all generously...
and it will be given to him.

JAMES 1:5

Father, You are a wonder to consider. Not
only do You hold all wisdom, You share
it—all I have to do is ask. You impart good
and godly judgment in times and ways
that help me know how to live. And I'm so
grateful because life gets very confusing.
Sometimes all I can do is stop and call
on Your name and wait for Your divine
intervention for getting through my maze
of circumstances. Thank You for not leaving
me to my own human logic. I want
to walk in Your way.

AMEN.

PRAISE FOR HIS PRESENCE

Be strong and courageous....
For the LORD your God will be with you
wherever you go.
JOSHUA 1:9 NIV

O Lord, how glad I am to know that You
are with me wherever I go. Wherever I go,
I can be strong and courageous. How can
I not be, knowing You are there?! I claim
this truth today and will not be afraid—
of people, of circumstances, of feeling
inadequate or inept. You are with me, and
You won't let me fall—that's a promise. All
praise to You for Your presence, because I
need You. In Your great name I pray.
AMEN.

PRAISE FOR HIS TRUTH

You are the God of my refuge....
Send Your light and Your truth;
let them lead me.

PSALM 43:2-3

Lord, I love Your Word and Your truth
because I know it's sound—it won't change.
And even though sometimes I don't like
learning truth about myself, I love learning
truth about You and Your love for me.
Help me let go of my earthly biases and
challenge me to trust You to think beyond
them. Expand my limited thinking and
perspectives with Your greater, eternal
thoughts. Push me out of my comfort
thinking and give me Your mind for holy
reflections. In Your great name I pray.

AMEN.

PRAISE FOR HIS POWER

His power is among the clouds....
The God of Israel gives power
and strength to His people.

PSALM 68:34-35

Father, some days can be so hard. But I
believe that the power You give, the power
I have through You, is far greater than any
mountain I face. I will overcome the fear I
face, I will work through the hardship one
moment at a time, and I will stand firm in
the hope of Your hand without wavering. I
draw from the power that is mine to take.
I feel so very glad for the victory I have in
You. All praise be to You.

AMEN.

PRAISE FOR A PURPOSE

It is God who works in you to will and to act
in order to fulfill His good purpose.

PHILIPPIANS 2:13 NIV

Lord, as I prepare for another day, help me
remember to keep Your purpose and plan
for my life as my greatest goal. Move my
feet, guide my thoughts, lead me through
the work before me, and remind me that I
am not my own. I am Yours to use however
You need in order to further Your kingdom
today. I feel so honored to be part of You
and a greater good in light of eternity. I
worship You with all my heart.

AMEN.

PRAISE FOR DELIVERANCE

I have trusted in Your faithful love;
my heart will rejoice in Your deliverance.

PSALM 13:5

Lord, I thank You now for delivering me—
from my past sin and mistakes, from the
consequences of my own eternal destiny,
and into the hope and promise of heaven.
Because of Your death and resurrection, I
am able to experience true peace and look
to the future with joy and pleasure. Your
faithfulness is true, and Your love is through
and through, and my heart overflows.

AMEN.

PRAISE FOR ETERNAL LIFE

God has given us eternal life,
and this life is in His Son.
The one who has the Son has life.

I JOHN 5:11–12

Father, thank You, thank You, thank You for Your Son, Jesus. Thank You that I can know Him personally, that I can receive His gift of life, not only here on earth but for forever. Thank You that life doesn't end here but will go on for eternity in Your very presence. This fills my heart with hope and strength to live here, today, to the fullest I am able, planting seeds of hope in others so they will come to know You too. In Jesus' wonderful and great name.

AMEN.

PRAISE FOR HIS ACCESS

For through him we both have access in
one Spirit to the Father.

EPHESIANS 2:18

Father, I love that I have full access to
You at any time, day or night. Your door
is never closed; I don't have to make an
appointment. I can approach Your throne
and pour out my heart to You and know,
without doubt or hesitation, that You are
not only there, You welcome me. Thank
You for hearing my cries, thank You for
receiving the outpouring of my heart day
after day. I run to Your arms now and soak
in Your loving presence to carry with me
wherever I go. In Your great name.

AMEN.

PRAISE FOR HIS LOVE

God proves his own love for us in that while
we were still sinners, Christ died for us.

ROMANS 5:8

Father, I am humbled and grateful to think
that You loved me before I ever loved You.
You sent Jesus to die for me before I ever
even knew who He was. You loved me
enough to pursue me, and now I get to
live each day, each moment, in the warm
and healing embrace that You give. I know
I don't deserve it—I get preoccupied and
wander down paths You're not on—yet Your
faithful love remains. It is the lifeline that
keeps me going, the very essence of what
sustains me. And I am so grateful.

AMEN.

PRAISE FOR UNENDING HOPE

Now may the God of hope fill you with
all joy and peace as you believe so that you
may overflow with hope by the power of
the Holy Spirit.

ROMANS 15:13

Father, today I am holding onto hope.
It's what keeps me filled with passion
and strength to move forward no matter
what. You are my encouraging hope when
discouragement knocks. You are my beacon
of hope for a way where there is no way.
You are my light of hope in a world filled
with darkness. You are my anchor of hope
on a planet that swirls with confusion.
Through the power of Your Spirit in me,
I hold onto hope. All praise be to You.

AMEN.

PRAISE FOR INTERCESSION

So Peter was kept in prison, but the church
was praying fervently to God for him.

ACTS 12:5

Father, when I see someone suffering or in
need and I don't know what to do, I love
that, at the very least, I can pray for them.
In fact, it's a pleasure and an honor to pray
for others You place in my path or lay on
my heart. I know You hear and respond
because I've felt times when others have
prayed for me when I've really needed it.
It is truly amazing how Your Spirit works
when we intercede on behalf of others.
Thank You for such a gift.

AMEN.

PRAISE FOR RENEWAL

He refreshes and restores my soul.
PSALM 23:3 AMP

Lord, I love that today is a new day. It's a
new life, a new joy, and a new hope yet to
be unveiled. You restore what got broken
yesterday and offer fresh starts in all the
todays going forward. Thank You that I
don't have to remain in past drudgeries,
I don't have to listen to old, negative
thoughts. I can step into this day with a
brand-new grasp of Your goodness to me
without hindrance. I praise You
and only You, almighty God.
AMEN.

PRAISE FOR AN UNCHANGING GOD

Every good and perfect gift is from above, coming down from the Father of lights, who does not change like shifting shadows.

JAMES 1:17

Father, in a world that changes, sometimes on a daily basis, I am so relieved and glad that You do not change. Your promises, Your love, Your faithfulness, Your wisdom— they are all the same now as they were in the beginning of creation. I hold on to You with all my might. I want to remain firm and steadfast in my spirit; I strive to remain unmoved by the whims of today's fads and false doctrines. You are my Rock and Redeemer, and I praise You for keeping me grounded and secure.

AMEN.

PRAISE FOR HIS COMPASSION

Lord, You do not withhold Your compassion
from me. Your constant love and truth
will always guard me.

PSALM 40:11

God, You know every detail of what weighs
on my life. You see my circumstances, and
You care. Your compassion is all around—by
the comfort and peace I feel in my heart,
and by the warm and tender ways You
minister to my spirit through Your Word
and through others. Thank You for being
so loving and kind to a heart that is bruised
from the challenges of this world. I know
that You are close and attentive to my cries.
I rest in You today.

AMEN.

PRAISE FOR HIS KINDNESS

God did this so that in the future world
he could show how truly good and kind
He is to us because of what
Christ Jesus has done.

EPHESIANS 2:7 CEV

Father, Your love reaches to the heavens,
Your faithfulness to the skies. And I rejoice
in the kindness You've shown through
the sacrifice of Your Son. If not for Jesus
and the thoughtfulness of Your ways, all
of humanity would be without hope and
without a future with You. You are pure
love, and I am humbled and grateful for
You, my God and Savior. In Jesus' name.

AMEN.

PRAISE FOR PRAYER

When You call out to me and come to Me
in prayer, I will hear your prayers.

JEREMIAH 29:12 NET

Father, thank You for not being a far-
off God. Thank You for the gift of prayer
and the way it brings me closer into Your
presence. I couldn't imagine what life would
be like if I couldn't talk to You about my
day and lift up my concerns and desires
to Someone who cares the way You do.
And thank You for answering my prayers,
for touching my life with blessing upon
blessing in ways only You would know to
do. With a grateful heart.

AMEN.

PRAISE FOR HIS GLORY

Finally...whatever is true, whatever is honorable, whatever is just, whatever is pure, whatever is lovely, whatever is commendable—if there is any moral excellence and if there is anything praiseworthy—dwell on these things.

PHILIPPIANS 4:8

Father, if I'm to think on whatever is true and honorable, just, pure, and lovely, I will simply dwell on You. You are all that is good, and Your splendor shines far above any earthly existence. The glory of Your presence leaves me speechless, and the glory of Your love leaves me wanting for nothing. Your wonder and beauty abound, and I am blessed to abide in the glory due Your name. In Jesus I pray.

AMEN.

NOVEMBER

GRATITUDE

GRATEFUL FOR NEW SEASONS

May [Joseph's] land be blessed by the Lord
...with the bountiful harvest from the sun
and the abundant yield of the seasons.

DEUTERONOMY 33:13-14

Father, fall brings a cool, windy breeze
and change of landscape that carries
excitement and renewal to my spirit. It's a
lovely reprieve from hot and dry summer
days. You do the same for my heart and life:
even though fiery trials prevail, I have the
constant hope of rest and refreshment and
for new ways to see Your majesty and glory.
I am grateful for and abide in knowing I can
count on Your faithfulness at every turn in
life's seasons. All praise be to You.

AMEN.

HIS LIGHT OF LOVE

When darkness overtakes him, light will
come bursting in. He is kind and merciful.

PSALM 112:4 TLB

Lord, this time of year generates extra
blackness and extended hours to the night
sky. But I see this as lovely because of the
extra beautiful backdrop it makes for Your
stars and galaxies to shine. The numerous
constellations, the planets and their
moons—they all radiate the beauty of Your
creation as a gift of mercy and forgiveness
You bring to a sinful world. I'm so grateful
for the light of hope You bring and the
reminder of Your constant and faithful love
to me. In Jesus' name.

AMEN.

COLOR IN WINTER

Every good and perfect gift is from above,
coming down from the Father of lights,
who does not change.

JAMES 1:17

Father, I am grateful for the gift of
evergreen trees. When all other trees
have lost their leaves to the grip of the
approaching winter, evergreens remain the
same—glowing with life. They portray Your
constant and unchanging presence and
provision for my physical needs as well as
my emotional and spiritual ones. No matter
how bleak the season I'm in, Your goodness,
Your blessing, Your love, and Your Spirit in
me remain the same. Because of this,
I will not be shaken. I will endure.
And I will not lose hope.

AMEN.

GRATEFUL FOR THE AROMAS OF LIFE

To God we are the fragrance of Christ...
an aroma of life leading to life.
II CORINTHIANS 2:15-16

Lord, fall smells are all around—bonfires
crackling, pot roasts simmering, apple pies
baking...They are a delight to the senses
and a comfort to take in. I can't help but
think of Your provision and goodness in my
life and how, in turn, I want to be a pleasing
aroma—a fragrance of Christ—that draws
people to You and fills their hearts with
a desire for more. Help me be a scent of
perfume and a spray of kindness
to those I meet today and every day.
In Your sweet name.
AMEN.

SEEKING HIS FACE

That kind of person receives blessings from the LORD.... That's how things are with the generation that seeks Him—that seeks the face of Jacob's God.

PSALM 24:5-6 CEB

Father, as I anticipate seeing friends and family during the upcoming holidays, I pause and anticipate seeing You in my every day. I just want to see You more. I want to be close through every minute, every situation I find myself in. Ultimately, I want to see You face-to-face for all of eternity. Until that time comes, I seek You.

AMEN.

REFLECTING ON HIS GOODNESS

I remember the days of old;
I meditate on all You have done;
I reflect on the work of Your hands.

PSALM 143:5

Father, the shortening of days and crispness
in the air make me want to reflect on Your
goodness and simplicity to be enjoyed—
squirrels gathering acorns, fire crackling
in the fireplace, geese honking and flying
overhead, and sitting still to quiet my
thoughts. I am grateful to ponder the rich
memories of Your faithfulness and the
abundance with which You have blessed me
now and over the years. I am truly thankful.

AMEN.

REST IN HIS CARE

But for you who fear My name [with awe-
filled reverence] the sun of righteousness
will rise with healing in its wings. And you
will go forward and leap [joyfully] like
calves [released] from the stall.

MALACHI 4:2 AMP

Father, the cooler weather and falling of
leaves brings a simple, childlike joy to my
heart. It's a season to retreat from the heat
of summer trials and rest in Your cool,
healing touch. My spirit wants to run and
jump with abandon into Your arms the way
I'd jump into a fresh piles of leaves. I know
You'd catch me and that I'd rest carefree
while gazing up at Your goodness.
I'm grateful to have such a sweet
and loving Lord.

AMEN.

GRATEFUL FOR HIS PROTECTION

Trust in Him at all times, you people;
pour out your hearts before Him.
God is our refuge.

PSALM 62:8

Father, just as my home provides refuge
from the harmful elements outside, You are
a refuge and place to rest my heart. I am
grateful for Your protection and for always
being a place of peace to run to. And just as
I decorate my home to reflect this season, I
am adorned by Your grace and loving care
in the seasons of my soul. You are my safe
haven. All praise and glory to You.

AMEN.

GRATEFUL FOR
LAYERS OF LOVE

He has clothed me with the garments
of salvation and wrapped me
in a robe of righteousness.

ISAIAH 61:10

Lord, as the weather gets cooler and I begin
to layer my clothes, wear a fall coat, and
wrap my neck with a scarf, I think of how
You clothe me with Your saving grace and
wrap me in Your redeeming love. You are a
garment of salvation for my soul, and You
protect me from the harsh elements of this
world. I am so grateful for Your care, and I
will carry this reminder in my heart today.

AMEN.

GRATEFUL FOR HIS FULLNESS

I have told you these things so that My joy
and delight may be in you, and that your
joy may be made full and complete
and overflowing.

JOHN 15:11 AMP

Lord, this cooler weather calls for a
steaming hot cup of cocoa, coffee, or tea.
Just thinking about it brings happiness and
comfort to my thoughts and mood. Filling
my mug makes gratitude rise in my heart
for the joy You bring into my life. I am filled
to the brim with Your simple goodness and
pleasure, and I am grateful.

AMEN.

GRATEFUL FOR GROWTH

So let it grow, and don't try to squirm out
of your problems. For when your patience is
finally in full bloom, then you will be ready
for anything, strong in character,
full and complete.

JAMES 1:4 TLB

Father I am grateful for growth. I'm the
same height on the outside, but, compared
to a year ago, I'm taller on the inside. It's
not been easy, but You've stretched and
grown my character, my patience, my faith,
and my trust to new levels. What used to
shatter my nerves no longer has the power
to rob me of the peace that You give. And I
find greater joy as I seek what brings
You joy. All praise to You.

AMEN.

GRATEFUL FOR HIS NEVER-ENDING LOVE

Neither death nor life...nor things present nor things to come, nor powers, nor height nor depth, nor any other created thing will be able to separate us from the love of God.

ROMANS 8:38–39

Father, I see it in relationships all the time— when trials come and days get difficult, someone leaves. So it's hard not to feel anxious about being abandoned, especially this time of year when family and friends are to gather, not split. But one thing brings solace: You will never leave. You promised. There is nothing I can do to turn away Your presence and Your love. I am so grateful for the comfort this brings. I love You, Lord.

AMEN.

GRATEFUL HE IS FOR ME

For the LORD your God is going with you!
He will fight for you against your enemies,
and He will give you victory!

DEUTERONOMY 20:4 NLT

Father, I'm grateful You are for me—You
fight daily on my behalf. At my beck and
call, You swoop in to guard and protect
me from the things I can see, and You
constantly battle in the realms I cannot
see. You hear my cries for help and ignite a
supernatural power and strength to see me
through every day. Thank You for winning
the battles of my mind so I can be in
perfect peace with You.

AMEN.

GRATEFUL FOR MY CHURCH FAMILY

After they arrived and gathered the church together, they reported everything God had done with them and that He had opened the door of faith to the Gentiles.

ACTS 14:27

Lord, how I love gathering together with other believers to worship and share in Your faithfulness and love. My church—Your church—is a safe haven to share from my heart and give and receive encouragement. I am so grateful to have such a place to gather, a place where I don't have to have my life together, because I rarely do! I come as I am, and I know that Your love and healing await. It is a wonderful gift, and I thank You.

AMEN.

GRATEFUL FOR HIS OMNISCIENCE

God is greater than our hearts,
and He knows all things.

1 JOHN 3:20

Lord, I am glad You know all things. I'm
glad You know my heart better than I do.
I'm glad You know how problems will turn
out and that You hold my future in Your
hands. I'm glad You are in control and that
You have more love than will ever fit into
my heart. I'm glad You are my God and that
You do not change. I'm glad to know I'll be
with You forever. Jesus, I am glad.
In Your sweet name.

AMEN.

GRATEFUL
HE CHEERS ME ON

Anxiety in a person's heart weighs it down,
but a good word cheers it up.
PROVERBS 12:25

Father, just as I cheer on my favorite
football team or a child's performance in
a school play, I know You are cheering me
on for building my faith and living with
integrity. I know because You lighten my
spirit and bring me great joy with each
whisper of love You speak into my life. So
the next time I feel anxious, help me to stop
and listen and receive the notes of gladness
You have waiting just for me. You know just
what to say, exactly when I need to hear it.
You are so good, and I love You.
AMEN.

GRATEFUL HE MEETS ALL MY NEEDS

Your Father knows the things you need
before you ask Him.

MATTHEW 6:8

Lord, when I think back on all the times
You've provided for my needs, I feel bad
that I don't trust You more to do the same
in my future. Why do I worry when You've
been nothing but beyond faithful to me?
Please forgive my anxious thoughts and
help me to rest in complete surrender to
Your way and Your power and Your plan for
meeting my needs today and in the days
ahead. In Jesus' name.

AMEN.

HIS WORD
ABOVE ALL OTHERS

The Son is the radiance of God's glory
and the exact expression of His nature,
sustaining all things by His powerful word.

HEBREWS 1:3

Lord, it's so easy to get confused by
conflicting stories in the news; it's hard to
know what is accurate. He said, she said,
and all is said with anger and hate. It's hard
to find anything that is sound and genuine
and shared in love. I'm so grateful I can turn
to Your Word and be brought to a place of
quiet and peace. Your Word is true, and I
can rest on that alone. Your Word sustains
all things, therefore I can stand secure and
not waver amid the confusion. Thank You
for being a steady force of truth.

AMEN.

GRATEFUL
HE KEEPS ME SECURE

We have this hope as an anchor
for the soul, firm and secure.
HEBREWS 6:19

Father, there are hurricanes, tornados, flash
floods, and high winds swirling around the
globe forcing people to evacuate homes
and flee for their very lives. This makes me
think of the times my circumstances flurry
out of control and create unstable ground
in which to rest my soul. But You, Lord, are
steady and secure—You guard and keep me
safe from giving in to a hopeless tomorrow.
You are my strong tower and keep me
anchored and fortified to live in confidence
and with courage. And I am grateful.
In Your great name.
AMEN.

GRATEFUL FOR HIS ABUNDANCE

Now to Him who is able to do above and beyond all that we ask or think according to the power that works in us...

EPHESIANS 3:20

Lord, this past year has had many challenges, but as Thanksgiving approaches I can't help but think about Your abundance in my life. You haven't just answered prayer and given blessings, You've shown up beyond measure. You've been faithful beyond what I even dreamed to ask or think. But that is Your way—You are mighty in all that You do, and You do everything to perfection. You will not be matched. I lift my heart with praise and thanksgiving.

AMEN.

GRATEFUL FOR THE LITTLE CHILDREN

Let the little children come to Me, and don't stop them, because the kingdom of God belongs to such as these.

LUKE 18:16

Jesus, I am grateful for each tiny colored handprint hanging on my refrigerator door. They bring pure and innocent life into my home. The lopsided flowers drawn off center outlast and outshine every bouquet on my table. The uneven heart shapes remind me that every heart is beautiful when it beats for You. A child's colorful mind poured out creates simple and beautiful masterpieces. They are a sweet glimpse of why You love little children. And I love them too. Thank You, Jesus.

AMEN.

GRATEFUL TO RECONNECT

If then there is any encouragement in Christ
...if any fellowship with the Spirit...make my
joy complete by thinking the same way,
having the same love, united in spirit, intent
on one purpose.

PHILIPPIANS 2:1-2

Lord, I am so grateful for family and friends
and time to reconnect and tell of Your
faithfulness. Sweet stories remind me that
You love my family even more than I do.
Difficult stories remind me that You are
sovereign over all, and in You I place my
trust. You watch over us when we're apart,
and You reunite us with the bond of love in
ways that are precious and priceless.
All thanks be to You.

AMEN.

GRATEFUL FOR HIS GOODNESS

You ascended to the heights.... He causes
the springs to gush into the valleys.

PSALM 68:18, 104:10

Lord, I am grateful for the joy of cooking
and baking, fellowship and football. Each
family dish carries stories of the past—a
walk through "remember when" that brings
nostalgic memories to life. The touchdown
roars and fumble gasps remind me of my
mountaintop moments and valley falls.
You've been with me in them all, and You'll
be with me in the ones to come.
Thank You for being a great, great God.

AMEN.

PERSISTENT IN HIS LOVE

Do not lack diligence in zeal;
be fervent in the Spirit; serve the Lord.
Rejoice in hope; be patient in affliction;
be persistent in prayer.

ROMANS 12:11-12

Lord, I am grateful for Your all-
encompassing provision, faithfulness,
lovingkindness, and hope—the same hope
the Pilgrims carried in their hearts as they
settled into a new land. Give me the same
courage, tenacity, and determination
never to give up, no matter how hard
circumstances may get. Help me to be a
shining example for the next generation to
keep the torchlight of Your love glowing
now until You call me home.

AMEN.

GRATEFUL FOR OUR SETTLERS

Teach [My commands] to your children,
talking about them when you sit in your
house and when you walk along the road,
when you lie down and when you get up.

DEUTERONOMY 11:19

Father, thinking back on the early settlers
of this country makes my heart swell with
gratitude—for their courage, bravery, and
endurance. Most of all I'm thankful for the
belief and trust they showed and for not
giving up hope. I am proud to carry on
their tradition of celebrating their faith
among their first harvest. They gave thanks
and acknowledgment to You, and it's a
tradition I want to carry on as well. You are
wonderful to provide such abundance both
then and now. All praise to You.

AMEN.

GRATEFUL FOR REST

He said to them, "Come away by yourselves
to a remote place and rest for a while."

MARK 6:31

Father, I am grateful for after-dinner strolls
that lead to oversized-chair naps. The
slower pace, the rest You give my soul in
this busy life is a respite I need and receive
to the fullest measure possible. This time
affords me space to rejuvenate my body
and fill my mind with quiet and peace. You
bring the deepest calm and sleep to a very
busy season. Thank You for time to rest in
Your presence, Lord.

AMEN.

MEANING IN THE COLORS

Every good and perfect gift is from above,
coming down from the Father of lights, who
does not change like shifting shadows.

JAMES 1:17

Father, I am grateful for pulling out tangled
Christmas lights to hang on the house. I
consider the colors of Your light in my life:
red for the blood You shed for me; blue
for the healing power of Your Word; green
for the new life You have brought and still
bring each day; white for Your pure and
holy Spirit; purple for Your royal robe of
sovereignty, wisdom, and devotion. Put
them together, and they are a splendid
diadem to behold the majesty of Your
throne. You alone are worthy of praise.

AMEN.

GRATEFUL FOR ME

You knit me together in my mother's
womb.... I have been remarkably and
wondrously made.

PSALM 139:13-14

Father, I am grateful that, as Your creation,
I can be totally me. That in Your eyes and
in Your care, I don't have to put on airs or
be anything other than who You've made
me to be. This is so freeing, and I'm grateful
that the only purpose I'm to fulfill is the one
You made me for. No matter how the world
says I should live, I am safe and confident in
Your plan for my life. Thank You for giving
me space and being a place where I can let
down all masks and walls
and know I am loved.

AMEN.

PASSING THE TORCH

In every situation [no matter what the circumstances] be thankful and continually give thanks to God; for this is the will of God for you in Christ Jesus.

I THESSALONIANS 5:18 AMP

Father, I'm so grateful for my life, just the way it is, bumps, bruises, holes, and all. Compared to less fortunate people around the world, I live as a queen. Help me look past superficial wants and spaces of my heart that seem empty. Fix my gaze on what I do have—a joy-filled life with meaning and purpose, Your hope and new mercies every day, and the love of a Father that carries me through each moment with grace and lovingkindness.
I am grateful for my life.

AMEN.

GOD'S NATURE
CAN BE MINE

Give thanks to the LORD, for He is good.
His faithful love endures forever.

PSALM 136:1

Father, I am filled with more gratitude
than I know how to express for Your
eternal nature. Your love, Your hope, Your
faithfulness, Your mercies—they are all
eternal promises that stand true forever.
They are a garland to wear around my neck
and claim as my own. I am truly grateful
knowing Your very essence resides in me.
You are breath, You are life, and I worship
You with all my heart. In Jesus' name.

AMEN.

DECEMBER

ADVENT

SOAK IN THE WONDER

Come and see the wonders of God;
His acts for humanity are awe-inspiring.

PSALM 66:5

Father, as I face the days and weeks leading
up to Jesus' birthday, remind me to pause
at times to simply soak in the wonderment
of the season: the sights, the lights, the
sounds, and the aromas...Give me the same
anticipation Mary and Joseph felt as they
approached Jesus' birth so the miracle of
that day remains at the forefront of my
mind and heart. In Jesus' precious name.

AMEN.

KEEP IT SLOW
AND SIMPLE

Remember the wondrous works
He has done, all His marvelous works,
and the justice He declared.
PSALM 105:5 CEB

.

Lord, I confess I feel anxious about the
season because of all the distractions that
call for my time, attention, and money.
They're diversions that point away from
You instead of to the miracle of Your
glory. Help me not to get swept up in the
trappings of materialism, overspending,
and overindulging. Help me to pace myself
and purpose to have a more simplistic
and meaningful celebration of Your birth. I
don't want to miss the true reason for this
wonderful time of year.

AMEN.

BE FILLED WITH COMPASSION

When He saw the crowds, He felt sorry
for them because they were hurting and
helpless, like sheep without a shepherd.

MATTHEW 9:36 NCV

Father, I know that this time of year is often
the most difficult for many people. Help
me to be sensitive to everyone I meet. Help
me to really look into peoples' lives, have
compassion on them, and show empathy
wherever it's needed. I want to be the
love of Jesus to broken hearts and extend
kindness to those who need a helping hand.
Help me to be a light of joy who just might
turn someone's difficult day into one that is
blessed. Glory to You in the highest.

AMEN.

COME TO THE QUIET

Faithful love and truth will join together;
righteousness and peace will embrace.

PSALM 85:10

Father, please take me away to a quiet
place today. I want to get away from the
noise in my head and the bustle all around
to be still and reflective of Your majesty. I
want to absorb the true gift of Jesus' birth
and what it means to this world and to
me. Keep me in a full awareness of Your
presence so I can capture the beauty that
beams throughout this wonderful time.
In Jesus' name.

AMEN.

A HUMBLE HEART

Be like-minded and sympathetic,
love one another, and be compassionate
and humble...giving a blessing,
since you were called for this,
so that you may inherit a blessing.

I PETER 3:8-9

Father, Christ was the ultimate example of
humility. He had to humble Himself to come
down to earth, be born in a manger, live as
a human being, and die on a cross. Please
give me a humble heart, too, to be ready to
act and to serve as Your Spirit leads. I want
to be a gracious touch in someone else's
day today, planting and spreading seeds of
Your love wherever I go. All glory to Jesus.

AMEN.

BE A BLESSING

Remember the words of the Lord Jesus
that He Himself said, "It is more blessed
to give than to receive."
ACTS 20:35 NET

Lord, making or shopping for gifts is
fun, but it's also a breeding ground of
temptation—of things I'd like to get for
myself. Help me keep You first in mind
along with the quick and ready desire to
be a blessing to others—not by buying
things so much as by giving what You give:
love, time, a listening ear, and small acts of
kindness. You gave Your life for me; help me
to give mine for Your glory and
Your good this season.

AMEN.

BURST FORTH IN SONG

My lips will shout for joy when I sing praise
to You because You have redeemed me.

PSALM 71:23

Lord, the carols from years past and the
new melodies that play out the heart of
Christmas also seize my heart of love for
You. Your joy is made complete in me when
I sing out words telling of Your birth and
the gift of salvation You are to a lost world.
I want my life to be a pleasing melody as I
lift my voice in worship and raise my hands
in praise. Joy to the world through You.

AMEN.

CLOTHED IN RIGHTEOUSNESS

My soul, bless the LORD! LORD my God,
You are very great; You are clothed
with majesty and splendor.

PSALM 104:1

Lord, just as You are clothed in majesty
and splendor, I want to be clothed in
righteousness this season. Give me an
upright spirit and a pure heart for spreading
goodness and cheer into others' lives. Make
me a lovely vessel for reaching out to those
who don't know or believe in You. Help me
point their eyes toward the manger, toward
Your birth, and toward Your gift
of salvation for eternity.

AMEN.

TAKE TIME TO REFLECT

Our Lord, I will remember the things You
have done, Your miracles of long ago.
PSALM 77:11 CEV

Jesus, I want to think and reflect on nothing
but You right now—what Your birth meant
to the world over two thousand years ago,
and the significance it still carries today.
You came to save us. You came to show us
what love is. You came to speak truth and
bring grace and show us the glory of God.
You came to die so that I would live. Jesus,
I will carry the beauty of Your essence in
my heart today as I meditate on the day it
all began—the day of Your amazing birth.
Hallelujah.
AMEN.

THOUGHTFUL GIVING

Peace I leave with you. My peace I give to
you. I do not give to you as the world gives.

JOHN 14:27

Father, as I think of gifts to give this year,
help me to be thoughtful of what truly
matters. Help me to know it's okay that
there are times when simply being present,
having sweet fellowship over a cup of
coffee, or going out of my way to help fill
a need often brings more meaning than
anything else. I pray that Your spirit of
peace within me shines steady and bright in
what can often be a stressful time for many.
As Your peace resides in me,
Your peace I give to others.

AMEN.

LET YOUR HEART SING

Sing a new song to the Lord!
Sing it everywhere around the world!

PSALM 96:1 TLB

I sing praise to You today, Lord! I ascribe to
You the glory due Your name, and I worship
You in the splendor of Your holiness. Your
mighty works and wonders are marvelous;
they are too numerous to count. May my
life be a song to You today, my actions a
sweet melody, and my thoughts a pleasing
aroma. This is a glorious time of year as I
count down the days until Your birth was
announced by the angels on high. I thank
You for this time and this moment to relish
the wonderful gift that You are.

AMEN.

REMEMBER HIS WORKS

I will also make every effort so that
you are able to recall these things
at any time after my departure.

II PETER 1:15

Father, I am so grateful for family traditions.
They remind me of Your faithfulness and
preserve memories to celebrate now. As
I prepare for Your special day, my heart
smiles from memories of family and friend
togetherness, as well as Your blessings over
the years. And You, God, have been very
faithful. I am filled with great hope for the
future, which fuels in me the desire to keep
serving You without wavering no matter
what. You are so good.

AMEN.

HOPE AMID THE MESS

Be strong and let your heart show strength,
all you who wait for Yahweh.

PSALM 31:24 LEB

Lord, You are hope in a hopeless world.
Without it, I would not know how to keep
living. You are my very breath and way of
strength, purpose, meaning, and ability to
carry out the calling You have placed on
me. The destruction and turmoil all around
could easily pull me down, but You raise me
high to keep and grow my faith until You
return. You are my one true hope amid the
mess. All glory to You.

AMEN.

HE IS JOY TO THE WORLD

In Your presence is fullness of joy.
PSALM 16:11 AMP

Lord, before knowing You, I didn't know the
meaning of joy. I thought it was a happy
feeling, but true joy runs so much deeper.
You have graced my life and my heart with
the ability to soar in the heights no matter
what is in my depths. It is a beacon that
shines from Your very nature and instills in
me—and in the world—the gift of hope that
only You can give. In Your presence, I have
joy to the fullest, and I am grateful.
Joy to the world!
AMEN.

A TASTE OF HEAVEN

For the bread of God is the one who comes
down from heaven and gives life to the
world.

JOHN 6:33 NET

Jesus, Your birth, Your life, Your death and
what they mean to this world are literally
a piece of heaven that God sent to earth.
You and Your goodness, Your pure and holy
love are a foretaste of what is to come in
the future. You, Your essence of heaven
will flow through my every heartbeat until
I close my eyes one final time and come to
be with You. Thank You for coming down.
Thank You for taking such a lowly position
so that I can be raised on high for eternity.
Thank You for saving the world.

AMEN.

BEAUTY IN OBEDIENCE

"I am the Lord's servant," said Mary. "May it
be done to me according to your word."

LUKE 1:38

Father, I can only imagine being in Mary's
place of trusting You with an immaculate
conception. Her obedience and grace are
an amazing example of following You,
going where You lead, doing as You say
when nothing around me makes sense. I
draw strength from her faithfulness and
belief that You are in control and that You
have a plan—a greater plan for my life than
I could ever dream.

AMEN.

LIGHT OF THE WORLD

I am the light of the world. Anyone who follows me will never walk in the darkness but will have the light of life.

JOHN 8:12

Jesus, how very dark this world, and my life, would be without Your light to shine through. You pierce into the deepest, darkest places of the soul and put Your Spirit and light in its place. You show which way to go; You light my way so I will not fall. You lift my spirit and fill it with joy. Help me to reflect Your light onto others this season, to draw in and to gather hearts that are hungry for hope and longing for healing. All praise and glory to You.

AMEN.

BREAD OF LIFE

"I am the bread of life," Jesus told them.
"No one who comes to Me
will ever be hungry."
JOHN 6:35

Father, as I enjoy all the treats and special meals with friends and family, make me mindful of the sustenance You provide when I cling to You. Help me not indulge in things that won't fulfill past the present moment but rather take You in for lasting pleasure and satisfaction. Fill each and every void so that cravings for the world disappear to where all I have and want is more of You. I hold You close to my heart.

AMEN.

HE LOVED FIRST

See what great love the Father has given us
that we should be called God's children.

I JOHN 3:1

Lord, Your love compares to no other.
It came down to save me before I even
believed in or cared about You. Your
love came first and wooed me in with an
embrace I couldn't resist. Your love covers
my sins, past and future, and makes me
Your own. Your love makes a way to spend
the rest of eternity with You. I cannot thank
You enough for loving me the way You do.
My heart is Yours because nothing equals
or comes close to what Your love has done
for me and for the world. I love You.

AMEN.

UNITY FOR THE NATIONS

Most of all, let love guide your life,
for then the whole church will stay together
in perfect harmony.

COLOSSIANS 3:14 TLB

Lord, just as You came to bring unity
among the Jews and the Gentiles, may we
have unity among the nations now. I pray
for peace around the globe to one day rule
over the fighting and destruction that is so
prevalent. May that peace begin with me—
to strengthen my family's bond, to be a
constant example that brings my neighbors
together, and to extend Your love to sisters
and brothers in our church body.
To You be all the glory.

AMEN.

HE IS KING

He is the blessed and only Sovereign,
the King of kings, and the Lord of lords.
I TIMOTHY 6:15

Father, I'm both honored and humbled to
think that the Spirit of the King of kings and
Lord of lords lives in me. Your very nature
resides within my heart, which makes me
pause and give great thanks. I worship and
adore You for the gift of Jesus' birth and
the power of His sovereignty. He is Heaven
Come Down, and I bow down to His majesty
and preeminence in my life. Hallelujah.

AMEN.

HE SEEKS OUT
THOSE HE LOVES

For the Son of Man has come to seek
and to save the lost.

LUKE 19:10

Lord, You not only came to save the lost
in this world, You came to seek them out
first. You actively looked for and sought out
me—a sheep that was as lost as lost can be.
And Your pursuit of love is relentless to this
day. Your grace abounds in every wrong
thought, rebellious act, and self-centered
agenda. And You make it clear that Your
love is faithful—nothing can separate me
from it. Who am I to deserve such a love?
You are a true gift—there is none like You.
You alone are worthy to be praised.

AMEN.

HEALING IN HIS WINGS

For you who fear My name, the sun of
righteousness will rise with healing in its
wings, and you will go out and playfully
jump like calves from the stall.

MALACHI 4:2

Jesus, Your birth, Your presence, Your Spirit
are all evidence of the supremacy of love
and a healing balm to a depraved world.
You give life to places that were once dead,
and You give joy and hope to hearts that
used to be empty and without purpose. No
other occasion compares to that of Your
birth. This world longed for something or
Someone to hope in, and You fulfilled that
longing. All my joyful praise to You.

AMEN.

ABIDE IN HIS PEACE

For a child will be born for us.... He will be
named Wonderful Counselor, Mighty God,
Eternal Father, Prince of Peace.

ISAIAH 9:6

Lord Jesus, with painful and chaotic times
in this world, I'm grateful to have Your
peace to hold on to. No matter what my
circumstances try to dictate, I am not
alone to face them. I can literally abide in
Your presence knowing that whatever my
surroundings look like on the outside, You
will remain a steadfast anchor of calm on
the inside. My challenges may be great, but
You are greater and over them all.
Thanks be to God for Your peace.

AMEN.

IMMANUEL—
GOD WITH US

Then she gave birth to her firstborn son,
and she wrapped Him tightly in cloth and
laid Him in a manger.

LUKE 2:7

O God, glory to You in the highest! I
celebrate Your arrival in the depths of my
heart. Thank You for coming down, for
living among humans, for sharing the glory
of the Father, and for covering me, and
this world, with Your grace. Your life gives
my life new meaning. I have purpose for
today and hope for the future. You are the
greatest gift this world has known, and
I embrace You with abandon. Hallelujah!
Praise and honor and glory to You.

AMEN.

PROCLAIM HIS COMING

The angel said to them, "Don't be afraid, for look, I proclaim to you good news of great joy that will be for all the people: Today in the city of David a Savior was born for you, who is the Messiah, the Lord."

LUKE 2:10-11

Father, thank You for sending Your Son, Jesus! Thank You for sending a Savior to walk among us and fulfill the prophecies of old to redeem Your people. Thank You for the wisdom, the teaching, the promises You have in place for each of us expressed through Him. Thank You for providing a way for all of us who believe to have eternal life with You. In His great name I pray.

AMEN.

CHOOSE TO FOLLOW HIM

And behold, the star, which they had
seen in the east, went on before them
[continually leading the way] until it came
and stood over the place where
the young Child was.

MATTHEW 2:9 AMP

Father, as the wise men followed the star to
where Jesus was born, I follow Your shining
light of love with all sincerity and passion.
You lead in the way of refreshing truth, and
Your presence of joy pierces my heart with
immeasurable effects. There is none like
You. You are the Savior of the world, and
You are my friend who only wants the very
best for me today and for eternity. I love
You and thank You for coming to this earth.
Glory in the highest.

AMEN.

MEDITATE ON HIS PRESENCE

Mary was treasuring up all these things
in her heart and meditating on them.

LUKE 2:19

Father, let me never get so caught up in the
hurriedness of life that I forget to pause and
dwell on the goodness of Your presence.
I love being still and meditating on what
You have done for the world and what You
have done for me. Jesus is a miracle of
redemption and saving grace in countless
ways, and I am so grateful beyond the
depths and honored to be called Your child.

AMEN.

OUR GREAT REDEEMER

[Anna] came up and began to thank God
and to speak about [Jesus] to all
who were looking forward to
the redemption of Jerusalem.

LUKE 2:38

Jesus, I thank You for being a God of
second, third, and numerous chances in life.
Thank You for taking time and talent I've
wasted and redeeming it for Your glory now
and in the future. Thank You for turning
what the enemy has meant for harm into
a life story that reveals Your power and
goodness. May I never be silent but always
speak about Your presence in my life, giving
You all the glory. You alone are worthy.

AMEN.

SOVEREIGN OVER ALL

Proclaim the LORD's greatness with me;
let us exalt His name together.

PSALM 34:3

Father, I praise Your name and Your
greatness. You are the One true God, and
I believe that You will remain sovereign
over all. You are absolute in a world that
is wasting away. You are supreme over
anything and everything that has ever
existed. It humbles me to know that You
love me, and yet You do. I exalt Your name
and give You all praise and honor.
Glory to You in the highest.

AMEN.

THANKSGIVING FOR ANOTHER YEAR

Goodness and faithful love will pursue me
all the days of my life,
and I will dwell in the house of the LORD
as long as I live.

PSALM 23:6

Lord, thank You for another year of life
and growth, lessons learned, and wisdom
gained. As I look back, I see Your loving
kindness and gentle mercies stamped all
over my days, and I feel grateful. Even with
the trials, I am glad. I am richer in love
because I know You more. You have been
faithful in the past, and now I pray for Your
faithfulness in the new year to come. In
Jesus' great name I pray.

AMEN.

LIVE YOUR FAITH

Dear Friend,

This book was prayerfully crafted with you, the reader, in mind—every word, every sentence, every page— was thoughtfully written, designed, and packaged to encourage you...right where you are this very moment. At DaySpring, our vision is to see every person experience the life-changing message of God's love. So, as we worked through rough drafts, design changes, edits, and details, we prayed for you to deeply experience His unfailing love, indescribable peace, and pure joy. It is our sincere hope that through these Truth-filled pages your heart will be blessed, knowing that God cares about you—your desires and disappointments, your challenges and dreams.

He knows. He cares. He loves you unconditionally.

BLESSINGS!
THE DAYSPRING BOOK TEAM

Additional copies of this book and
other DaySpring titles can be purchased
at fine bookstores everywhere.
Order online at <u>dayspring.com</u>
or
by phone at 1-877-751-4347